C000004638

THE
SOUTH WEST
Way

1995

THE COMPLETE GUIDE
TO THE SOUTH WEST COAST PATH,
GREAT BRITAIN'S LONGEST TRAIL.

THE SOUTH WEST WAY ASSOCIATION

Registered as a charity (No. 266754)

The Association formed to promote the interests of users of the South West Way (South West Coast Path)

CHAIRMAN

Brian Panton, 5 Nicholas Gardens, Ensbury Park,
Bournemouth BH10 4BA
Tel: (01202) 526954

TREASURER

Derek HEXTER, F.C.A.,
43 Torquay Road,
Newton Abbot,
Devon TQ1 2JB.
Tel: (01626) 52162

SECRETARY

Eric WALLIS
'Windlestraw',
Penquit,
Ermington,
Devon PL21 0LU,
Tel: (01752) 896237

MEMBERSHIP SECRETARY

Mrs Mary MACLEOD
1 Orchard Drive,
Kingskerswell,
Newton Abbot,
Devon TQ12 5DG.
Tel: (01803) 873061

Published jointly by:
The South West Way Association and Peninsula Press Ltd
P.O. Box 31, Newton Abbot, Devon TQ12 5XH.

Trade Sales and Distribution:
Hamlet Distribution, Moretonhampstead, Devon TQ13 8NA

© South West Way Association 1995

Printed in England by Leicester Printers Limited.

ISBN 1 872640 29 X

Originated by Greenshires Icon, 84 Longbrook Street, Exeter, Devon.

Jacket design by A&B Creative Services, Kingskerswell, Devon.

Jacket photograph of The Warren, near Noss Mayo
by Eric Wallis

CONTENTS

The production of this annual guide has been made possible by the support of the Countryside Commision for the Association's computer facilities.

COUNTRYSIDE COMMISSION

INTRODUCTION

The South West Way is one of the official long distance trails funded by the Countryside Commission and maintained on its behalf by County Councils and National Park authorities. The route is waymarked by the distinctive acorn symbol.

The South West Way is by far the longest of the Official Long Distance trails; it runs from Minehead in Somerset right round the South-Western peninsula to South Haven Point on the south side of Poole Harbour in Dorset. We ourselves reckon this is 613 miles, others differ but all agree it is a fair step! A recent contour count indicates you will climb over 91,000 ft which is three times Mount Everest.

This Footpath Guide attempts to provide in one single unit all the basic information you need to walk the path. The information is updated annually and members (see Invitation to Membership, page 112) are advised by Newsletters of important changes during the year.

We try to provide the basic information, that is sometimes so difficult to assemble for other Long Distance trails, in just one small booklet.

The path was enacted in the National Parks and Access to the Countryside Act of 1949. It must seem amazing therefore, to those who do not know the fact, that it is still unfinished after forty years.

It is sometimes called the South-West Peninsula Coastal Path, which is more of a mouthful. Parts of it are disguised as the Somerset and North Devon, North Cornwall, South Cornwall, South Devon and Dorset Coastal Paths. None of this administrative nonsense was intended by the originators of the path and walkers may find such divisions a nuisance. More to the point, these, and even smaller administrative divisions have been allowed in the past to spawn very different standards of routing and maintenance. However, now that The Heritage Coast Service and footpath wardening is becoming more universal, standards are improving all around.

A survey established that one of the chief joys of those accomplishing the Pennine Way was the sense of achievement; of a challenge met. What of our path which is twice as long and requiring far more total effort? More seriously because of its length, few will be able to undertake to walk it as a whole. That is why as much as possible of this guide is written to be just as useful to those who only wish to walk parts of the path.

The path does undoubtedly pass through some of the finest coastal scenery in Europe and, with its enormous variety and contrast between bustling resort and quiet cove, is a never ceasing source of delight. Its other main feature is the tremendous amount of interest of all kinds along its way.

This path is the longest Long Distance Trail – we think it is the finest we hope you will too! We certainly know of no other Long Distance Trail that has as much contrast and variety as ours. Try it!

THE OTHER WAY ROUND

In this book the description of the South West Way is from Minehead–Land's End–Poole. The Association has now written a description of the Trail for those walking the other way. It deals only with the path so this annual guide will be necessary for all the other information. The 'other way round' supplement is available from the membership secretary or secretary at £2.30 including postage.

WEATHER

The South West Way is more exposed to wind than any other Long Distance Trail – Pay attention to gale forecasts as well as rain. Along some sections, strong winds can be dangerous especially when rounding exposed headlands and crossing bridges. A high backpack can act like a sail. Detailed forecasts are available on: (01898) 500 405 (Somerset) / (01898) 500 404 (Devon & Cornwall) / (01898) 500 403 (Dorset),

A WORD TO BEGINNERS

Long Distance Path Walking

Please, these words are not for those hardy veterans who have all the gear, have done several paths already, and know all about it. We will only say to them at least read the second paragraph of 'Grading' near the beginning of the 'Trail Description' section. However, we do get a number of letters each year from those who have not ventured before on Long Distance Paths and need some advice. This we are pleased to try and provide and we do hope those who read this will find it helpful. However, it is easy to miss out things that folk wish to know, so if you who are new read this, and are still baffled, please write to us and we will try to provide the answers. As well as perhaps helping you, it will enable us to improve this section for another year and so be of help to more people.

For Those Who Have Never Been Walking

Have you been walking at all before? If the answer is no, do not for heaven's sake try and plan several days' continuous walking. You need to do some day walks – there are some very good ones on the coast – first. Better still, look for the sections marked "Easy" – start at one end and stop and turn back before you have half had enough. We say before half because it is always better to do a bit less and really enjoy it.

You can soon progress to setting out to walk a whole section either by using two cars or using public transport. One point here – if possible use the public transport to go out and walk back to your car or base. This means that you do not get yourself in a position of having to race the clock if you should take a bit more time than you thought.

If you are walking on your own, do please take additional care for, as you will appreciate, if you fall or twist an ankle there can be problems. If you are on your own therefore, you should leave a note with someone to make sure that you arrive at your destination. Not everyone is happy walking on their own and can feel lonely. There is also an added problem that you may try to do too much, so please bear this in mind.

There is no need to buy expensive equipment for the easy sections at the start. A pair of stout shoes and a rainproof is all you need. As you progress, a small rucksack or haversack for 'eats' will be needed next.

Obviously if you can join a walking club and go out with them you will collect lots of friendly advice on all sorts of gear you may care to purchase as you become more serious about walking. Maps, guides, etc., are all listed in their appropriate sections.

For Those Who Have Walked, But Not On Long Distance Trails

Day walking on Long Distance Trails is really no different from any other kind of day walking. It is only when you contemplate several days' continuous walking that other considerations arise and there are some pitfalls which even quite experienced day walkers often overlook.

Do not be too ambitious in the mileage you plan. Do not carry too much weight of gear.

Having stated the two big points, we will elaborate. You will not be able to accomplish in daily mileage the same amount you normally cover in a day walk! You will have to settle for less! The first reason is that you will be carrying more equipment; you must for instance, have a complete change of clothing and footwear, possibly nightwear and toilet kit. For this you need a bigger rucksack so you will be carrying quite a bit more weight than you normally do. Secondly, there is what we call the 'wear' factor. For the first few days until you are really fit, it is just simply more tiring having to walk each day. The last point could be called the 'interest' factor. Usually, if you are walking a Long Distance Path, you are further from your home base in fresh fields and pastures new; there is more to see so you will need more time to look around.

If you usually accomplish 15 miles a day – aim, say, for 12. This is particularly important if you are booking ahead. You can find yourself tied to a treadmill which you cannot get off. Booking ahead has the advantage that you know there is a bed ahead. On the other hand, it does mean even if you are tired, have developed blisters, and the weather is diabolical, you have to go on! Be guided too by our 'Trail Description' section, the terrain you are tackling. 6 miles, say, of a 'Severe' section can equal in effort 10-12 miles of an 'Easy' one.

We have stated you must carry more gear and this is true. Having said that, think long and hard about every item you imagine you may need. You will be surprised – you may find you will not want it at all! Watch particularly those extras such as cameras and binoculars – they are often a source of considerable weight. One little additional point, many rucksacks, even modern ones, are not as waterproof as you think. A plastic liner which can be obtained quite cheaply from rambling shops, etc., as an additional inner layer may save you that most unpleasant discovery after a long day spent in the rain that your only change of clothing is no longer dry. We would also recommend that in addition to this liner your dry clothing should then be enclosed in further plastic bags to ensure dryness. Trainer shoes are useful for wearing at the end of the day and can be worn on some parts of the path.

A sensible idea before undertaking a full Long Distance Footpath holiday is to take, say, a long weekend of two or three days first, walking continuously as a practice.

We are sometimes asked if you require a map as well as a guide book and our advice is certainly yes. A good guide such as Bartholomew gives you a considerable amount of information but, strange as it may seem, it is at its most useless when you actually get lost! Agreed, one does not get as badly lost on the Coastal Path as you can on inland ones but nonetheless a map is an asset. Furthermore many walkers derive much interest from looking at their route in relation to the rest of the countryside on ordinary walks and the same applies just as much, if not more so, on a Long Distance Path. The National Trail Guides offer a partial solution with their maps; but even these are not as useful as a Map Sheet.

Another point to watch especially on our Coastal Path is the availability of refreshment. At main holiday times, you will get it nearly everywhere except for the few places we especially mention in our 'Trail Description' section. Out of season, you will find it in surprisingly few places on long stretches of coast. The usual remarks about carrying stand-by supplies, therefore, certainly apply; better to carry an extra couple of bars of chocolate than to go hungry.

BADGES

We offer specially designed badges for the South West Way.

Cloth badges for rucksack, anoraks, etc. £1.00 inclusive of postage and packing

We think these badges are attractive – we hope you will too. Available both for members and non-members alike.

CERTIFICATES

These are now available to persons who have walked the whole path. Free to members. £1.25 to non-members.

BOOKS, etc.

This list is not exhaustive, there are a number of other books available but we have tried hard to list all those which are really useful and even those not really useful that you might think would be!

VIDEO

Aerial Britain – The South West Coast. Produced by C21C at £12.99. Available at all branches of W.H. Smith. This is the one we helped to make. Beautiful – The coast path from a helicopter.

PUBLICATIONS ARE AVAILABLE DIRECT FROM YOUR ASSOCIATION, FOR QUICK SERVICE PLEASE WRITE TO THE MEMBERSHIP SECRETARY, MRS M. MACLEOD, 1 ORCHARD DRIVE, KINGSKERSWELL, NEWTON ABBOT, DEVON TQ12 5DG.

South West Way – Minehead to Penzance

South West Way – Penzance to Poole.

Both these excellent pocket sized books are by Martin Collins. We can recommend them as most useful. Available from Cicerone Press, 2 Police Square, Milnthorpe, Cumbria, LA7 7PY at £8.95 each (Postage and packing 55p per book). Also available from the South West Way Association.

National Trail Guides – published by Aurum Press in association with the Countryside Commission and Ordnance Survey. Available from the Countryside Commission Publications, Printworks Lane,

Levenshulme, Manchester M19 3JP; The Ordnance Survey, Romsey Road, Maybush, Southampton SO9 4DM; most bookshops and our own association from the Membership Secretary. These are good guide books with good maps. An excellent venture by the producers involved.
Minehead to Padstow by Roland Tarr
Padstow to Falmouth by John Macadam
Falmouth to Exmouth by Brian Le Messurier
Exmouth to Poole by Roland Tarr
Price £9.99 + 50p postage from our Membership Secretary.

500 Mile Walkies by Mark Wallington (from bookshops only). £4.99 Published by Arrow.
An amusing account of a walk by the author, accompanied by a dog, along the whole of the path.

Walk the Cornish Coastal Path by John Mason. This is a Bartholomew Map and Guide at £5.99. An excellent guide to all of the Cornish Coast. From Membership Secretary (Post 50p).

South West Cornwall Guide including accommodation, available free from: The Tourist Information Centre, 79 Meneage Street, Helston, Cornwall. Tel: 01326 565431.

Eleven Walks in West Cornwall. Price £1.00 plus postage from the Tourist Information Centre, 79 Meneage Street, Helston, Cornwall. Tel: 01326 565431.

Discover Guides – Praa Sands, St. Keverne, Coverack, Mullion and Redruth Town Trail. Free of charge. Send SAE to Tourist Information Centre, 79 Meneage Street, Helston, Cornwall. Tel: 01326 565431.

LANDFALL WALKS BOOKS – Bob Acton of Devoran has written eleven splendid books that contain well over 100 circular walks in Cornwall. These feature sections of the coast path throughout the county. They will enable walkers to progress along the coast path by basing themselves at one location. Write to Landfall Publications, Landfall, Penpol, Devoran, Truro, TR3 6NW for full list, or telephone 01872 862581.

Footpath Touring with Ken Ward. Land's End and The Lizard. Price £3.75 including postage. Available direct from 'Sea Chimney', South Down, Beer, EX12 3AE. An excellent guide to this section of the path by one of the co-authors of the well-known Letts Guides.

Walk South Devon Coastal Path and Dartmoor by John Mason and Eric Hemery. This is a Bartholomew Map and Guide at £5.99. An excellent guide to the South Devon Coast. Available from Membership Secretary (Post 50p).

Two Moors Way (now illustrated) – by Devon Area Ramblers Association – Price £2.70. This is not our path. One is enough! But we do stock the Official Guide. This describes the path from Lynmouth in North Devon to Ivybridge near Plymouth – and very well done it is too. (Available from South West Way Association. Postage 40p. Write to Membership Secretary.)

The South Devon Coast Path. An Aerofilms Guide featuring spectacular aerial photo-maps and landscapes covering the walk from Lyme Regis to Plymouth. Price £8.99. Published by Ian Allen Ltd, Terminal House, Shepperton, Surrey, TW17 8AS (01932 228950).

SOUTH WEST WAY ASSOCIATION PUBLICATIONS

Path Descriptions by our association are very detailed accounts on all aspects of short sections of the coast path and include maps and illustrations. They cover in great detail what cannot be included in the guide book.

These Path Descriptions are all priced at 75p + 19p postage for up to 2 copies, 29p for up to 4 copies, 36p for up to six copies and 43p for up to 12 copies. All are available from the Membership Secretary, Mrs M. Macleod, 1 Orchard Drive, Kingskerswell, Devon, TQ12 5DG. Telephone: (01803) 873061.

PATH DESCRIPTIONS

NORTH DEVON AND SOMERSET

Minehead to Lynmouth
Lynmouth to Ilfracombe
Ilfracombe to Croyde Bay
Croyde Bay to Appledore
Appledore to Hartland Point
Hartland Point to Marsland Mouth

(List continued overleaf.)

CORNWALL

Marsland Mouth to Crackington Haven
Crackington Haven to Tintagel
Tintagel to Port Isaac
Port Isaac to Padstow
Padstow to Porthcothan
Porthcothan to Newquay
Newquay to Perranporth
Perranporth to Portreath
Portreath to Hayle
Hayle to Zennor
Zennor to Sennen Cove
Sennen Cove to Porthcurno
Porthcurno to Penzance
Penzance to Porthleven
Porthleven to The Lizard
The Lizard to Helford
Helford to Falmouth
Falmouth to Portloe
Portloe to Mevagissey
Fowey to Looe
Looe to Cremyll (River Tamar)

SOUTH DEVON

Plymouth (River Tamar) to Wembury
Warren Pt. Wembury to Bigbury
Bigbury to Salcombe
Salcombe to Torcross
Kingswear (River Dart) to Brixham
Brixham to Shaldon
Shaldon to Sidmouth
Sidmouth to Lyme Regis

DORSET

Lyme Regis to Abbotsbury
Abbotsbury to Weymouth
Weymouth to Lulworth Cove
Lulworth Cove to Kimmeridge
Kimmeridge to South Haven Point

HISTORICAL

The South West Way 125 Years Ago
The Queen v Ames (1840-3). A Legal
Marathon on the Devon/Dorset border

All Long Distance Footpaths

There used to be a dearth of information about Long Distance Footpaths. This is not the case today so we do not list as many addresses as we used to do.

The best basic information on literature available on All Long Distance Footpaths is the Ramblers' Association, 1/5 Wandsworth Rd. London SW8 2XX.

We can also recommend the Long Distance Walker's Handbook: 4th Edition: Completely revised and updated by John Margetts. Contact – Brian Smith, 10 Temple Park Close, Leeds, West Yorkshire LS15 0JJ (01532 642205).

THE NATIONAL TRUST 'COAST OF CORNWALL' LEAFLETS

A series of detailed leaflets, with maps, covering the coastline owned by the National Trust in Cornwall. Each leaflet contains information of the history, flora and fauna of the area as well as general information on points of interest.

They are available from National Trust shops in Cornwall or from the Cornwall Regional Office, Lanhydrock, Bodmin, Cornwall PL30 4DE (please include a donation to cover postage):

No 1	Bude to Morwenstow	70p
No 2	Crackington Haven	50p
No 3	Boscastle	70p
No 4	Tintagel	70p
No 5	Polzeath to Port Quin	60p
No 6	Bedruthan and Park Head	60p
No 7	Crantock to Holywell Bay	60p
No 8	St. Agnes and Chapel Porth	50p
No 9	Godrevy to Portreath	60p
No 10	West Penwith: St. Ives to Pendeen	80p
No 11	West Penwith: Cape Cornwall to Logan Rock	70p
No 12	Loe Pool and Gunwalloe	70p
No 13	The Lizard, West Coast	70p
No 14	Kynance Cove	60p
No 15	The Lizard, East Coast	70p

No 16	The Helford River	70p
No 17	Trelissick	70p
No 18	The Roseland Peninsula	60p
No 19	St Anthony Head Battery	60p
No 20	Nare Head and the Dodman	70p
No 21	Fowey	80p
No 22	East Cornwall: Lantic Bay to Sharrow Point	70p

NATIONAL TRUST REGIONAL INFORMATION OFFICES:

Devon Information Office, Killerton House, Broadclyst, Exeter, Devon EX5 3LE (Tel: Exeter (01392) 881691).

Dorset & Somerset Region Information Office, Stourton, Warminster, Wilts. BA12 6QD (Tel: Bourton, Dorset (01747) 840560).

Cornwall Information Office, The Estate Office, Lanhydrock Park, Bodmin, Cornwall PL30 4DE (Tel: Bodmin (01208) 74281).

RAILWAYS

Throughout the year there is an excellent service of direct InterCity trains between London (Paddington) and Torbay, Plymouth and Cornwall. There are also regular InterCity Cross Country services linking Birmingham, the North West, the North East and Scotland with Torbay, Plymouth, Cornwall, Bournemouth and Poole. All these services have catering facilities available for the whole or part of the journey. During May to September, InterCity services are considerably augmented on Saturdays (check your local railway station) and seat reservations are essential on many of these trains to avoid overcrowding and ensure passengers a comfortable journey (Direct InterCity trains between London (Paddington) and Torbay run <u>only</u> in the summer timetable as do InterCity services to Newquay).

All daytime services between Paddington, Plymouth and Penzance are operated by InterCity 125 trains with the journey time to Torquay and Plymouth just over 3 hours from London.

There is also a regular Wessex Electric service from London (Waterloo) to Bournemouth, Poole and Weymouth for those who intend to walk the Dorset end of The South West Way. East Devon is served by a two-hourly Network Express service from Waterloo to Axminster (for Lyme Regis and Seaton) and Honiton (for Sidmouth). Now with new class 159 trains.

Regional Railways have greatly improved their service in the South West and can now offer a direct new Class 158 link between Paignton and Cardiff. The new Class 158, air-conditioned 90mph trains also link Penzance with South Wales, Birmingham and Swindon. New rolling stock has been introduced on most branch lines in Devon and Cornwall and make reasonable connections into and out of the long distance InterCity services. Most of these branch lines are open on Sundays during the summer months and the first four also have a limited Sunday service during the winter months.

Westbury–Yeovil–Weymouth	Liskeard–Looe
Exeter–Barnstaple	Par–Newquay
Exeter–Exmouth	Truro–Falmouth
Newton Abbot–Torquay–Paignton	St Erth–St Ives
Plymouth–Gunnislake	

A wide variety of attractive reduced-rate fares are often available in the popular holiday areas during the summer months as are a wide variety of Rover tickets. Details of these may be readily obtained on enquiry at stations and Travel Centres.

Private Branch Line Railway

Bishops Lydeard to Minehead – The West Somerset Railway PLC run steam trains through twenty scenic miles to Minehead. Bishops Lydeard is four miles outside Taunton and easily accessible by bus. The service operates between March and October. For details contact the company at 'The Station', Minehead TA24 5BG (Tel: 01643 704996).

Paignton to Kingswear (Dartmouth) – For the rambler who is also a railway enthusiast, the Paignton and Dartmouth Railway is a 'must'. This most attractive line runs from Paignton to Goodrington,

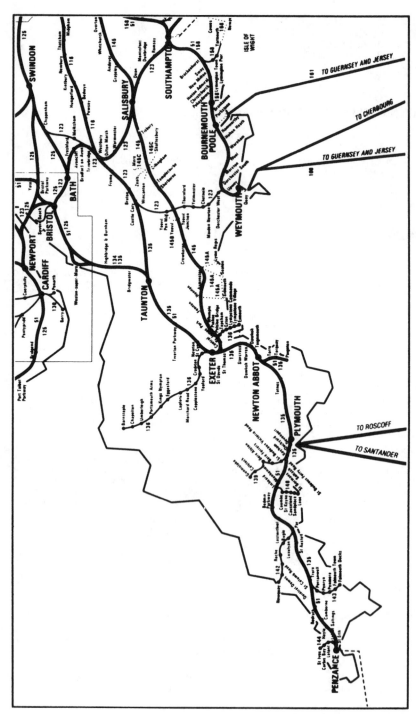

1365/SW 63	Camborne (South)/Hayle	1363/SX 74/84	Kingsbridge/Stoke Fleming
1364/SW 33/43	St Ives & Penzance (North)	1358/SX 85/95	Dartmouth & Brixham
1368/SW 32/42	Land's End/Newlyn	1351/SX 86/96	Torbay
1369/SW 52/62	Helston & Prussia Cove	1342/SX 87/97	Newton Abbot & Teignmouth
1372/SW 61/71	Lizard Point	1330/SY 08/18	Sidmouth
1370/SW 72/82	Helford River	1316/SY 29/39	Lyme Regis/Axminster
1366/SW 83	Falmouth & St Mawes	1317/SY 49/59	Bridport
1361/SW 94/SX 04	Mevagissey & Tregony	1331/SY 58	Abbotsbury
1354/SX 05/15	St Austell & Fowey	1343/SY 67/77	Weymouth/Portland
1355/SX 25/35	Looe	1332/SY 68/78	Weymouth (North)/
1356/SX 45/55	Plymouth		Dorchester (South)
1362/SX 54/64	Newton Ferrers & Thurlestone	1333/SY 88/98	Wareham
1367/SX 73	Salcombe	1334/SZ 08	Studland/Brownsea Island

Outdoor Leisure Maps

There are three Ordnance Survey Outdoor Leisure Maps 1:25,000 available for parts of the path. These are South Devon (No. 20), Purbeck and South Dorset (New edition – Double sided) (No. 15). And double sided map (No. 9) – Exmoor.

As far as the South Devon one is concerned, we cannot really recommend it to anyone. There is so much of the South Devon Path which is missing and the fact that the Brixham peninsula is shown as an inset makes it difficult to use.

The Purbeck and South Dorset double sided map is excellent and covers the entire stretch from West Bay (Bridport) to South Haven Point at the mouth of Poole Harbour. The Exmoor map is also excellent.

Where an area of a Pathfinder map is completely covered by an outdoor leisure map, then the Pathfinder map may not be available.

Altos Explorer Series

Penwith–Land's End – Map Guide – £3.75. The Coast Path from St Ives to Penzance. Clear, large scale and all paths clearly marked. available from membership secretary.

OFFA'S DYKE: MORE THAN A PATH!

For 1,200 years the term 'Offa's Dyke' has meant the great earthwork thrown up by the powerful ruler of Mercia (central England) to mark the boundary with the Welsh and as such it has also colloquially come to refer to the Anglo-Welsh boundary. In the last forty years a new meaning has come to the term with the designation of the Offa's Dyke Long Distance Footpath in 1949. It took ?? years from designation to the opening in 1971 and here lies the origin of another meaning ? Dyke', the Association. This was originally set-up to act as a pressure group to pu??? sary works and the opening to take place. Since 1971 Offa's Dyke Path has ?????? ?e best used of the National Trails, and a name known to most 'serious' w??? ??on has had no mean success itself with, now, over 1,000 members.

But why have a long distance footpath along thi? ??? ??e historic border it may be but it follows no obvious physical feature. Of?? ???walking route is something else, in one word, Variety. The Welsh Border ? ??country and some of the most attractive and unspoilt moorland, rolling h??? ???crossed by the Path between the tourist areas of the Wye Valley and the Nor?? ???Across the plains of Gwent, over the Black Mountains, the river valleys and hills of R???, the Severn and Dee valleys, the limestone hills round Llangollen and the Clwyddian ridges: the list of varied attractions is long. For nearly half the route the earthwork is your companion, often 20 feet from ditch to top even after twelve centuries of erosion. Many castles and abbeys lie near the route and though the 177 miles can be covered in a week, most visitors will sensibly prefer a more leisurely walk.

But why an Offa's Dyke Association? And, in particular, what was the need for this voluntary pressure group to continue beyond the official opening of the Path? We foresaw some of the needs of visitors to the Path that official facilities and services could not meet and we correctly anticipated a minor boom in walking and other tourism where there had been little before. Also inevitably there would be a different approach to the Path from walkers and from historians, from visitors and from those who lived and worked there. If we could cover this range of interests then harmony in development, rather than areas of conflict would be more likely.

We run the Offa's Dyke Centre at Knighton, which also serves as the town's T.I.C., and thus receives some local authority aid. It helps nearly 30,000 people each year. Most want to know about accommodation and so we publish annual 'where to stay' and camping lists. Additionally we issue guides, 'strip maps' of the route, point to point route notes in both directions, circular walks and alternative routes based on the Path, also town trails and history notes. We sell non-ODA maps and guides. Association members were commissioned to write the 'official' guides to the Path. Finally, we send a wide-ranging journal three times a year to members.

Maintenance and erosion of the Path with the attendant problem of vandalism, are constant sources of concern. We have a system of volunteers, each watching over a stretch of the route and negotiating with farmers over access etc., and local authorities over necessary maintenance; even doing minor works themselves. Since 1982 this work has been in co-operation with an 'Offa's Dyke Development Officer' (ODDO); this venture is financed by the Countryside Council for Wales and works via Powys County Council from our Knighton Centre.

We are pleased to be regarded as a body to be consulted on policy matters by national and local government and their agencies.

A strong membership and flourishing sales are the key to our public recognition and to our strength as a pressure group: please write, with S.A.E., to Offa's Dyke Association (S.W.), West Street, Knighton, Powys, Wales. Tel: 01547 528753.

ERNIE KAY – Publications Officer

BANKS

We suggest you contact your own bank for a list of where their branches along the trail are located. Probably a Girobank account would prove to be the most convenient as there are small Post Offices in most villages.

TELEPHONES

We urge you to consider buying BT Phonecards or chargecards for use in the larger towns. Life is easier when you do not have to seek change for a call box.

RIVER CROSSINGS

The walker tends to view his feet as the only certain method of progress – and why not? Unfortunately, the absolute purist would need to be an olympic-class swimmer not to have to use ferries on the South West Way. However, a certain amount of scepticism is helpful, absolute reliance on ferries is not advised!

There are other ferries available on the Path which walkers may wish to use for diversions or short cuts. We have attempted to list those directly necessary.

Tide Tables

The tide tables included in this edition refer to the times of low water at Devonport. These tables will act as a guide for those wishing to wade across the Gannel (Newquay), Gillan Creek, and the Erme and Avon (Bigbury on Sea). Please be sure to read the warnings given under each section. We have been criticized for being too cautious over the times we suggest for wading the rivers, and know that some walkers cross at other times. We believe our attitude is correct as there are certainly dangers, but you may wish to try at low tide on other occasions to see if conditions will permit a *safe* crossing. Variations in barometric pressure can affect tide levels. Remember there are different levels daily of low water, if in doubt seek local knowledge.

| Newquay (The Gannel) | Deduct 30 minutes | Gillan Harbour | Deduct 15 minutes |
| R. Erme | As at Devonport | Bigbury/Bantham (R. Avon) | As at Devonport |

* The following Tide Tables are Crown Copyright. Produced from Admiralty Tide Tables with the permission of the Controller of Her Majesty's Stationery Office.

MARCH 1995
From 26th March add 1 Hour for BST

Days	Low Time a.m.	Low Time p.m.
1 W	1157	–
2 Th	0016	1239
3 F	0056	1317
4 Sa	0132	1351
5 Su	0204	1421
6 M	0232	1448
7 Tu	0258	1513
8 W	0323	1538
9 Th	0352	1613
10 F	0452	1735
11 Sa	0624	1901
12 Su	0744	2016
13 M	0855	2122
14 Tu	0953	2215
15 W	1042	2302
16 Th	1127	2346
17 F	1210	–
18 Sa	0027	1251
19 Su	0107	1330
20 M	0145	1406
21 Tu	0223	1443
22 W	0301	1522
23 Th	0345	1609
24 F	0440	1711
25 Sa	0558	1850
26 Su	0750	2031
27 M	0908	2136
28 Tu	1004	2227
29 W	1051	2312
30 Th	1134	2353
31 F	1214	–

APRIL 1995
Add 1 Hour for BST

Days	Low Time a.m.	Low Time p.m.
1 Sa	0031	1250
2 Su	0105	1322
3 M	0136	1351
4 Tu	0203	1416
5 W	0228	1440
6 Th	0250	1501
7 F	0316	1532
8 Sa	0402	1638
9 Su	0542	1820
10 M	0704	1936
11 Tu	0813	2042
12 W	0914	2140
13 Th	1008	2232
14 F	1057	2319
15 Sa	1143	–
16 Su	0004	1228
17 M	0048	1311
18 Tu	0130	1352
19 W	0212	1433
20 Th	0255	1516
21 F	0341	1604
22 Sa	0437	1705
23 Su	0550	1829
24 M	0722	1959
25 Tu	0838	2106
26 W	0935	2159
27 Th	1023	2245
28 F	1106	2326
29 Sa	1145	–
30 Su	0004	1222

MAY 1995
Add 1 Hour for BST

Days	Low Time a.m.	Low Time p.m.
1 M	0038	1253
2 Tu	0109	1322
3 W	0136	1348
4 Th	0203	1414
5 F	0229	1441
6 Sa	0258	1514
7 Su	0342	1606
8 M	0457	1733
9 Tu	0621	1853
10 W	0731	2001
11 Th	0834	2103
12 F	0933	2200
13 Sa	1027	2252
14 Su	1117	2341
15 M	1206	–
16 Tu	0030	1254
17 W	0117	1340
18 Th	0204	1426
19 F	0251	1512
20 Sa	0338	1559
21 Su	0430	1653
22 M	0529	1756
23 Tu	0639	1912
24 W	0754	2025
25 Th	0857	2124
26 F	0950	2214
27 Sa	1035	2257
28 Su	1115	2336
29 M	1152	–
30 Tu	0011	1226
31 W	0044	1256

JUNE 1995
Add 1 Hour for BST

Days	Low Time a.m.	Low Time p.m.	Days	Low Time a.m.	Low Time p.m.
1 Th	0115	1326	16 F	0155	1416
2 F	0145	1357	17 Sa	0242	1501
3 Sa	0216	1428	18 Su	0327	1545
4 Su	0249	1503	19 M	0411	1629
5 M	0328	1547	20 Tu	0458	1718
6 Tu	0420	1646	21 W	0551	1816
7 W	0530	1802	22 Th	0654	1926
8 Th	0646	1918	23 F	0805	2039
9 F	0755	2027	24 Sa	0909	2139
10 Sa	0900	2131	25 Su	1001	2227
11 Su	1000	2229	26 M	1045	2309
12 M	1055	2323	27 Tu	1124	2347
13 Tu	1148	–	28 W	1201	–
14 W	0015	1240	29 Th	0022	1235
15 Th	0106	1329	30 F	0057	1309

JULY 1995
Add 1 Hour for BST

Days	Low Time a.m.	Low Time p.m.	Days	Low Time a.m.	Low Time p.m.
1 Sa	0130	1342	16 Su	0225	1443
2 Su	0203	1415	17 M	0305	1522
3 M	0236	1449	18 Tu	0344	1559
4 Tu	0311	1527	19 W	0422	1638
5 W	0352	1613	20 Th	0503	1724
6 Th	0444	1714	21 F	0555	1824
7 F	0555	1833	22 Sa	0659	1939
8 Sa	0717	1954	23 Su	0817	2058
9 Su	0832	2108	24 M	0925	2157
10 M	0940	2212	25 Tu	1016	2243
11 Tu	1040	2310	26 W	1059	2324
12 W	1135	–	27 Th	1138	–
13 Th	0003	1227	28 F	0002	1216
14 F	0054	1316	29 Sa	0038	1252
15 Sa	0141	1401	30 Su	0113	1326
			31 M	0146	1359

AUGUST 1995

Add 1 Hour for BST

Days	Low Time a.m.	Low Time p.m.
1 Tu	0219	1432
2 W	0252	1508
3 Th	0328	1549
4 F	0413	1641
5 Sa	0514	1755
6 Su	0642	1930
7 M	0815	2055
8 Tu	0929	2202
9 W	1030	2259
10 Th	1123	2350
11 F	1212	–
12 Sa	0037	1258
13 Su	0121	1340
14 M	0202	1418
15 Tu	0238	1453
16 W	0311	1525
17 Th	0343	1558
18 F	0417	1638
19 Sa	0503	1734
20 Su	0608	1849
21 M	0725	2012
22 Tu	0845	2125
23 W	0946	2215
24 Th	1032	2257
25 F	1113	2337
26 Sa	1152	–
27 Su	0015	1230
28 M	0052	1306
29 Tu	0126	1340
30 W	0159	1414
31 Th	0232	1450

SEPTEMBER 1995

Add 1 Hour for BST

Days	Low Time a.m.	Low Time p.m.
1 F	0309	1530
2 Sa	0351	1620
3 Su	0449	1733
4 M	0620	1918
5 Tu	0807	2048
6 W	0922	2153
7 Th	1019	2246
8 F	1108	2333
9 Sa	1153	–
10 Su	0017	1236
11 M	0058	1315
12 Tu	0134	1350
13 W	0208	1422
14 Th	0237	1451
15 F	0305	1520
16 Sa	0332	1552
17 Su	0408	1646
18 M	0519	1807
19 Tu	0643	1928
20 W	0803	2043
21 Th	0909	2140
22 F	1000	2225
23 Sa	1044	2307
24 Su	1125	2347
25 M	1205	–
26 Tu	0026	1244
27 W	0104	1321
28 Th	0140	1358
29 F	0216	1436
30 Sa	0254	1518

OCTOBER 1995

Until 21 Oct add 1 Hour for BST

Days	Low Time a.m.	Low Time p.m.
1 Su	0339	1610
2 M	0437	1723
3 Tu	0609	1911
4 W	0755	2035
5 Th	0906	2136
6 F	1001	2226
7 Sa	1048	2311
8 Su	1131	2353
9 M	1211	–
10 Tu	0031	1249
11 W	0106	1322
12 Th	0137	1352
13 F	0205	1420
14 Sa	0230	1446
15 Su	0253	1511
16 M	0318	1552
17 Tu	0413	1723
18 W	0559	1846
19 Th	0718	1957
20 F	0826	2057
21 Sa	0922	2149
22 Su	1011	2235
23 M	1056	2319
24 Tu	1140	–
25 W	0002	1223
26 Th	0044	1305
27 F	0125	1346
28 Sa	0205	1429
29 Su	0248	1515
30 M	0335	1608
31 Tu	0433	1717

NOVEMBER 1995

Days	Low Time a.m.	Low Time p.m.	Days	Low Time a.m.	Low Time p.m.
1 W	0554	1848	16 Th	0456	1754
2 Th	0728	2008	17 F	0627	1909
3 F	0840	2110	18 Sa	0739	2013
4 Sa	0936	2201	19 Su	0841	2111
5 Su	1024	2246	20 M	0937	2203
6 M	1107	2327	21 Tu	1028	2252
7 Tu	1146	–	22 W	1117	2340
8 W	0004	1223	23 Th	1204	–
9 Th	0039	1256	24 F	0026	1252
10 F	0109	1326	25 Sa	0113	1339
11 Sa	0136	1354	26 Su	0159	1426
12 Su	0202	1421	27 M	0245	1513
13 M	0228	1448	28 Tu	0332	1603
14 Tu	0255	1523	29 W	0423	1659
15 W	0337	1625	30 Th	0525	1808

DECEMBER 1995

Days	Low Time a.m.	Low Time p.m.	Days	Low Time a.m.	Low Time p.m.
1 F	0642	1926	16 Sa	0518	1809
2 Sa	0800	2035	17 Su	0645	1926
3 Su	0904	2132	18 M	0759	2033
4 M	0957	2219	19 Tu	0905	2134
5 Tu	1042	2301	20 W	1004	2230
6 W	1123	2340	21 Th	1058	2323
7 Th	1200	–	22 F	1150	–
8 F	0014	1235	23 Sa	0013	1241
9 Sa	0046	1306	24 Su	0103	1331
10 Su	0115	1336	25 M	0151	1418
11 M	0144	1405	26 Tu	0237	1503
12 Tu	0213	1435	27 W	0320	1547
13 W	0243	1507	28 Th	0404	1632
14 Th	0318	1548	29 F	0450	1722
15 F	0407	1647	30 Sa	0545	1823
			31 Su	0658	1942

SUGGESTED ITINERARY

For some the fun of planning their own itinerary is a major part of the enjoyment of their holiday. If you are one of these DO NOT READ THIS SECTION.

On the other hand there are folk who have been put off tackling our path because they just could not see how to pack over 600 miles walking into a normal holiday. The answer is, of course, you cannot! Offa's Dyke or the Coast to Coast Walk, to take just a couple of examples, work out well in a fortnight. Other paths such as The South Downs or The Ridgeway conveniently occupy a week.

Our Path, we reckon, needs about seven weeks to accomplish. That being so, we have tried to divide it up sensibly into seven roughly equal sections. Obviously, if we are going to suggest weekly stages, the beginning and end of each one must have reasonable accommodation and public transport. That presents a problem in itself; so after some thought we have broken it down into six 7-day and one 6-day week. As usual, we would be very glad to hear from anyone who has tried one of our weeks and to hear their comments on it.

If you are a seasoned walker then there is a lot to be said for walking the whole path albeit at different times in our usual anticlockwise order. However, if you are not experienced, then obviously we should point out that the South Cornwall week, the fourth one in our schedule, is much the easiest if you want to start with something less demanding.

To keep the weeks set out below in a simple format the information is only an outline. IT IS ESSENTIAL TO CONSULT THE DETAIL IN THE REST OF THE GUIDE TO EFFECTIVELY PLAN YOUR HOLIDAY. Mileages can vary depending on where you actually stay! Furthermore, our mileages are only approximate because they are all "rounded".

Kilometres	Miles	
		Week 1 (Seven days)
		MINEHEAD B.R. Taunton W. Nat. Minehead (not Sundays or Bank Holidays). Direct coach service from London.
14	9	PORLOCK or PORLOCK WEIR
21	13	LYNMOUTH/LYNTON
21	13	COMBE MARTIN
21	13	WOOLACOMBE
28	17	BRAUNTON
18	11	INSTOW
16	10	WESTWARD HO! W. National Barnstaple/B.R. Exeter
139	86	
		Week 2 (Seven days)
		WESTWARD HO! B.R. Exeter W. National Barnstaple
18	11	CLOVELLY
16	10	HARTLAND QUAY
22	14	BUDE
27	16	BOSCASTLE
21	13	PORT ISAAC
27	17	TREVONE
27	17	NEWQUAY B.R. Newquay
158	98	
		Week 3 (Six days)
		NEWQUAY B.R. Newquay.
18	11	PERRANPORTH
20	13	PORTREATH
28	17	ST IVES
21	13	PENDEEN WATCH

24	15	PORTHCURNO
18	11	PENZANCE B.R. or National Coach
129	80	

Week 4 (Seven days)

		PENZANCE B.R. or National Coach
21	13	PORTHLEVEN
22	13	THE LIZARD
18	11	COVERACK
20	13	HELFORD
16	10	FALMOUTH
20	13	PORTLOE
19	12	MEVAGISSEY St Austell B.R.
		St Austell/Mevagissey Western National
136	85	

Week 5 (Seven days)

		MEVAGISSEY St Austell B.R.
		then bus service (Western National)
18	11	PAR
21	13	POLPERRO
21	13	PORTWRINKLE
21	13	PLYMOUTH (Cremyll Ferry)
22	14	WEMBURY POINT
22	14	BIGBURY ON SEA
21	13	SALCOMBE B.R. Plymouth
		W. National Kingsbridge–Salcombe
146	91	

Week 6 (Seven days)

		SALCOMBE B.R. Plymouth
		W. National Kingsbridge–Salcombe
20	13	TORCROSS
16	10	DARTMOUTH
18	11	BRIXHAM
18	11	BABBACOMBE
24	15	DAWLISH WARREN
19	12	EXMOUTH (via Topsham Ferry, see appropriate
		section for Starcross Ferry)
21	13	SIDMOUTH B.R. EXETER. Bus – Devon General
		Exeter–Sidmouth
136	85	

Week 7 (Seven days)

		SIDMOUTH B.R. Exeter
		BUS Devon General
15	9	SEATON
23	14	SEATOWN (Dorset)
19	12	ABBOTSBURY
23	14	WEYMOUTH
19	12	LULWORTH
21	13	WORTH MATRAVERS
23	14	SOUTH HAVEN POINT Ferry-Sandbanks, Wilts &
		Dorset to Poole or Bournemouth, B.R., National
		Express Coach from Bournemouth to
143	88	London/Cheltenham

THE SOUTH WEST WAY

General

This is a series of notes on the state of the path which we hope will help you in your walking. Obviously it is very difficult to keep something as extensive as this both up-to-date and concise. Suggestions for improvement or amendments will always be welcome. We can only keep you right up-to-date with the state of the path if YOU will keep us posted about conditions as you find them on any stretch of the path. Your fellow members will be grateful, and so will we!

If you have any complaints about ordinary maintenance or signposting on the path, please write either to the Exmoor National Park Authority or the relevant County Council, Devon, Cornwall or Dorset. They should see this is done, and what is generally not realised is that any work carried out is 75% Grant aided from Central Government for official Long Distance Footpaths such as the South West Way. If you have any major problems or difficulties we would always be glad to be advised as well.

The comments are based on the Ordnance Survey Landranger series (1:50,000 maps). These Landranger Map numbers are shown where they cover a fair stretch of each section. The reference numbers down the side are our own and are simply inserted to help quick reference in any correspondence, etc.

Towns and villages are now marked T or V respectively but the places at the end of each section appear as the first entry in the next one. We obviously stick our necks out to try and classify towns and villages. To us a town should have a reasonable range of shops, maybe even something as exotic as a laundrette! Villages should at least have a pub and a village store open all the year round, and a bus service. There are, of course, numerous other places yiou can get refreshment in season, but precious few out of it. Please note that all sections end at reasonable access points, usually having parking facilities.

Places which can be reached by rail are marked.

Distances: Explanatory Notes

The distances shown are in four columns:

> The first column is the distance of the section to the nearest kilometre.
> The second column is the cumulative distance in kilometres.
> The third column is the distance of the section to the nearest mile.
> The fourth column is the cumulative distance in miles.

We aimed to keep the actual distances in a simple form and not pretend to a degree of accuracy that is not inherent in them. To this end we have rounded every section to the nearest kilometre or nearest mile and we have done the same to the cumulative distances.

Members will notice that our estimate of the total mileage of the route has shot up from 570 to 613 miles. We have always said it was longer than any of the authorities' ideas. With the advent of National Trail Guides, the Ordnance Survey have now made an official distance estimate – 594 miles. We have examined this figure closely. They do not include the City of Plymouth or Topsham Ferry to Exmouth. These have to be walked if one intends to cover the whole official route. Bearing in mind the whole path we feel 613 miles is nearer to the total than their 594.

The distances are of course, always marked along the Oficial Path, however bad a route it may be, unless we tell you to the contrary at the beginning of the section in the Footpath Guide.

Grading

Each section is graded as Easy, Moderate, Strenuous or Severe. Please note we no longer take into consideration lack of escape routes, distances from public transport, etc. It is purely a question of physical difficulty. We will try to highlight in the sections other considerations when they apply.

We would like to underline one point; the whole of our path is certainly not easy. Some parts of it are but other parts are not. We have had a number of letters from people who have walked The Pennine Way and who have been literally amazed at the severity of some of our tougher sections! Perhaps as a further comment we may add that recently we walked two 6 mile adjacent sections. The time taken for one was 50% more than the time taken for the other. This may give additional emphasis to the importance of studying terrain if you wish to compute time.

TAXIS

Coast Path walking can be be arduous in places but some of the hard work can be eliminated. We have been informed that the use of local taxis can ease the tired muscles. Transport is not for the walker naturally but for Rucksack transfer from B&B to B&B. Local taxi firms will be pleased to give a price for the service. Consult yellow pages or ask the locals for details of taxi operators.

THE OTHER WAY ROUND

In this book the description of the South West Way is from Minehead–Land's End–Poole. The Association has now written a description of the Trail for those walking the other way. It deals only with the path so this annual guide will be necessary for all the other information. The 'other way round' supplement is available from the membership secretary or secretary at £2.30 including postage.

THE TRAIL DESCRIPTION – Minehead to Poole
(FOLLOW THE ACORN WAYMARK)
Remember – we now have a Poole to Minehead Guide Book

FOOTNOTES

In certain sections we have added footnotes commenting on nine books where you may be led astray. These are as follows:

'BMG' – John Mason's Bartholomew Map and Guide Books.
'CP' – Martin Collins' two South West Way books by Cicerone Press.
'NTG' – Four National Trail Guides – published by Aurum Press in association with the Countryside Commission and the Ordnance Survey.
'AFG' – Aerofilms Guide,

1	Minehead to Porlock Weir	OS 181 (T) Minehead

Grading: Official Route – Moderate	Distance –	14	14	9	9
Alternative – Strenuous					

See also our Minehead to Lynmouth path description

The official path does not start where you would expect it to at the western end of the sea front road. Look for an inconspicuous opening between two cottages on the sea front a little to the east of the harbour.

Keen photographers please note the splendid official signs have unfortunately not been put at the start of the path. There is one on the opposite side of the road on the promenade and one 100 yards after you have started. Nonethless, if you want your picture by a sign you had better get it here. Despite their promises the Countryside Commission have still not provided one at the other end at Poole Harbour, so do not postpone your photo 'til you get there – it would be a long way to go to be disappointed.

The official route, although a good moorland walk, does not follow the traditional coastal route. Strong walkers, looking for something better, can start at the westerly end of the sea front road, proceed via Greenaleigh Farm to Burgundy Chapel and then make a steep ascent up North Hill. An easier alternative to this first piece is at Greenaleigh Farm, immediately before the house and the signpost 'To Burgundy Chapel and Beach' to fork left and then turn back, sign post 'North Hill'. This path zigzags back to pick up the official route so avoiding the steep climb after Burgundy Chapel.

When taking the steep ascent from Burgundy Chapel at the T junction go left, the path to the right goes only to a view point, and at the next junction go forward.

When you have gained the summit of North Hill, there is a sign, with the acorn, pointing to Selworthy and Bossington. Follow the line of this until you come to the next coast path sign, where there is a right fork marked 'Rugged Cliff Top Path'. Ordinary walkers should proceed forward on the official route but the more adventurous can fork right and proceed working seaward by what is a well defined path.

The 'Rugged Cliff Top Path' is a splendid alternative to the official path with good views to seaward and is well marked with yellow waymarks and warning signs 'No Dogs'. At the second stile take the left fork and soon follow the rough track down by a boggy stream to the bottom of the unnamed Combe at 937 481. From here take the well-defined diagonal path leading up the hill to the wall which is the National Trust boundary. This wall can be followed towards the sea at first and then along parallel to the sea all the way to Western Brockholes. After Western Brockholes the path swings inland but is well signposted and rejoins the official path behind Hurlstone Point.

Those who have taken the official route, when reaching Bossington Hill should take the definitive right of way which goes around Hurlstone Point rather than the signposted official route. This much more spectacular and, apart from gale force conditions, is not at all unsafe despite warning signs. If you stay on the official path take care to descend the path to the left of Hurlstone Point and do not be tempted to take the more obvious path to the left (no signpost) contouring round Bossington Hill.

The official path wanders inland from Hurlstone Point via Bossington and then out to the sea again. It is usually possible, except in conditions of extreme flooding, to walk all the way along the beach, until you have passed the river, turning slightly inland there to pick up the path, so saving oneself a laborious detour. Look for the path leading down to the eastern end of the beach; the beginning of this can be found 30 yards north of a seat on the path and slightly to seaward. There is a stile within 10 yards. The beach route will save you just over half a mile walking. Please note that there is no path at all at the western end of Porlock Beach although one is shown on sheet 181 of the Ordnance Survey Map. It is fairly clear going from east to west.

NTG does not mention the beach route to Porlock Weir.

2	Porlock Weir to Lynmouth		OS 181 and 180

Grading: Moderate	Distance –	21	35	13	22

See also our Minehead to Lynmouth path description

The official path leaves Porlock Weir behind the Anchor Hotel. We prefer the route in front of the Anchor Hotel which stays on the seafront a little longer, turning left at sign marked Culbone.

1991 brought bad news for this section. At Worthy you will be confronted by an Exmoor National Park notice warning walkers travelling towards Culborne Church on the official route to use the path with great care due to a further landslip possibility. You have the choice of the woodland official route or the marked diversion. It is impossible to predict this landslide. By the time you read this there could well have been one during the last winter whilst this book was at the printers. We do not agree with the National Park Authority on their choice for a future route and are pressing for a better permanent diversion when the area becomes too hazardous or when the slip occurs

You proceed from Porlock Weir by field paths to Worthy. At Worthy you go through an arch and take a woodland path up towards Culbone, going under a second low arch. Shortly afterwards you come across a diversion caused by a large landslip. You then have to follow signs to Culbone usually with red or yellow patches or waymarks in addition. You come to a bridge at Culbone running over another footpath below. Immediately after the bridge you rejoin the official path and if you wish to see the interesting church you have to turn right to go down to the churchyard. The path itself goes forward and although it is now the official path it is not always consistently marked and has not always got acorns. The sign at the beginning says 'Coast Path Lynmouth'. Just a few days before this book went off to the printer we heard that the old 'official' path has been reinstated through Culbone Wood into Yenworthy Wood. After a five year geophysical study Exmoor National Park have waymarked and cleared the path so continue to follow blue waymarks (or blue and yellow) and the Acorn symbols when you see them, and signposts: Sisters Fountain, later Wingate Combe and, of course, Lynmouth.

For those who wish, there is a permissive but not definitive path which keeps closer to the coast and in our opinion is better. To take this, follow the instructions above to well beyond Culbone, you will pass Silcombe and Broomstreet Farms then turn right when you reach the second sign to Glenthorne Beach. Go down through the Pinetum and then at the second sign to the beach turn left instead of right. At the next turning right, then left just above Glenthorne House, you pass a turreted building on your left which once served as a garage and come to an unusual arch on a hairpin bend. There is a lion on top of the arch and birds on top of the turrets. There is an arrow forward to the coast path and sign on the actual signpost says Wingate Combe. Go through this arch and follow the zig-zag path up till you come to another path crossing at an angle where you turn right and you are now back on the official path.

At Caddow Combe, the official route is again signposted inland 'Countisbury 1¹/₂ miles'. The sure-footed will prefer the right of way signposted 'Lighthouse' which proceeds out to the Foreland Point Lighthouse. Just before the entrance to the lighthouse where the wall commences on the right, the path takes off up the bank to the left. The beginning is clearly marked because the authorities tell you they no longer maintain the path.

The National Trust have a good path which can be taken down the seaward side of the main A39 coastal road so avoiding the upper reaches of Countisbury Hill. You then have a few yards on the main road but if you keep a sharp lookout you can again escape from the traffic by turning right off the road and descend to the foreshore through the woods.

You come out on the foreshore. Walk along into Lynmouth crossing the footbridge, there turn right down to the seafront turning left up the steps before the cliff railway, that is assuming you are a purist and are not actually going to use the railway which you can well do if you wish! If you use the railway you do suffer slightly at the top in that you will have to walk nearly into Lynton and then out again to regain the North Walk. After all, it serves you right for not having walked the whole way!

| **3** | **Lynmouth to Combe Martin** | **OS 180 (T) Lynton/Lynmouth** |

Grading: Strenuous   Distance –   21   56   13   35

See also our Lynmouth to Ilfracombe path description

Please note there is a long, lonely section onward from Heddon's Mouth to Combe Martin without any chance of refreshment.

The path itself out from Lynton is a Victorian idea for a coastal footpath called the North Walk and although to our modern ideas tarmac might not be the ideal footpath medium, it is a very fine high level walk indeed. This takes you very happily out to Castle Rock. Unfortunately, the official route is then on road all the way through to Woody Bay. However, there are diversions which will save you some road walking. The first takes off to the right after the turning circle (roundabout) at the end of the Valley of Rocks and then goes in a loop back, to come out by the Lodge at the beginning of Lee Abbey.

The second alternative is a left turn immediately opposite Lee Abbey which is labelled 'Woodland Walk' (each end) and rejoins the road about three-quarters of a mile further along.

This is one of the finest pieces of coastal path in North Devon and should not be missed by anyone who is reasonably sure-footed, or unless weather conditions are very bad. The path takes off just before the Woody Bay Hotel opposite the Red House and the beginning of the path is marked by a signpost on the right which says 'Public Footpath to Woody Bay Beach ³/₄ mile'. This path comes out on another road where you turn up left. There will be another sign 'Footpath Hunters' Inn 2¹/₄ miles'. You will cross a stile with a sign 'Heddon Valley Hunters' Inn'. This is a superb path which is now the new official route. It is much nearer the coast giving splendid views. This path later descends to the floor of the valley and you should turn left along the river, signposted 'Hunters' Inn ¹/₂ mile', until you get to the lower of the two footbridges. Then you cross the river, and soon turn left, walk ¹/₄ mile upstream to a gate. Turn sharp right and take a zig-zag path half way up to where there is a wooden bar across the path. Here you turn right towards the sea and wonderful views at Peter Rock. (In strong winds you could step over that wooden bar, continue up the zig-zag then turn seaward at the top). From Peter Rock the route takes a seaward path to East Cleave. Walkers who have been this way before will certainly appreciate the improvement in the official route from Woody Bay Hotel to East Cleave. It was always our recommended alternative route. Needless to say, whilst in the valley of Heddon's Mouth, those requiring refreshment have easy access to the Hunter's Inn.

Just west of East Cleave you will regain the old official route passing along High Cliff and North Cleave. Another of our recommendations has now been implemented. At map reference 625

482 take the short walk across open heathland to avoid the walk up to the old Trentishoe Down Road. As there are many sheep tracks by Sherrycombe we suggest you follow the grass track along the top of the combe to the inland end of it to pick up the path down.

When ascending Great Hangman from Sherrycombe you reach a seat. Keep alongside the wall on your left. There are a number of well-walked paths going out to the right but they are all wrong! From Great Hangman the path is clear to Little Hangman where more stunning views are available.

When you come to the shelter above Combe Martin, turn right on the unmarked path. This has the better views.

C.P. – The official route no longer goes to Hunters Inn and Trentishoe. See fourth paragraph above.

4	Combe Martin to Ilfracombe Harbour		OS 180 (T) Combe Martin		

Grading: Moderate	Distance –	9	65	5	40

See Also our Lynmouth to Ilfracombe Path Description

The path leaves the Kiln car park up Seaside Hill Road above the beach. Turn right onto a narrow tarmac lane, which climbs steeply to rejoin the main A399 road.

Walk on the slightly raised path along the road side, through two gates, then along a path at the top of the fields, to a flight of wooden steps.

Turn left at the top onto a slip road to join the new section of the A399. Walk along the side of the road on a path, up hill for about 250 yards, turn right just past a bus shelter. Then down hill on a road to cross over the now disused section of the A399, into a lane by the side of the Sandy Cove Hotel. This lane becomes a tree lined track until you can see a high stile on the right. Climb this and you are onto open fields with a sight of the sea again. Watermouth Castle, built 1825, comes into view. At Watermouth it is possible to cross the foreshore at low tide to a flight of steps. Take care the rocks can be slippery. This is not possible at high tide when one has to continue along the road with no pavement for approximately 30 yards and there is then a stile off right into the woods. The next section of the path is very pleasant on the western side of Watermouth and now happily continues out and around Widmouth Head. This new section provides some very spectacular walking; we particularly commend the view back from Widmouth Head over Watermouth, whatever the state of the tide or sea. This will be your last good view point of the dramatic setting of the Great Hangman and the Little Hangman eastwards above Combe Martin. After Widmouth Head the path continues in front of the coastguard cottages going to Rillage Point.

After Rillage Point, site of some old limestone quarries, this fine section ends up on the coast road again with a walk towards Hele Sands then up some steps. The path then zig-zags up steps with impressive viewpoints. At Beacon Point there is a fine view of Ilfracombe. The path gets a little lost at the top of Hillsborough but all paths here do end up in the town.

5	Ilfracombe to Lee		OS 180 (T) Ilfracombe		

Grading: Easy	Distance –	5	70	3	43

See also our Ilfracombe to Croyde Bay Path Description

Walk along the edge of the harbour, bear left at the slip and then right into Broad Street. At a T-junction, turn left into Capstone Road next to the Sandpiper Inn. After about 150m (170 yards), turn right and walk around Capstone Point. The route through the town is well waymarked with blue coloured Devon County Council signs.

Follow the coast around Wilders Mouth beach, along the promenade, in front of a parking area. Turn inland, then climb steeply behind some gardens above the Museum. You are now in Granville Road. Pass through a gate, turn right, walk along this cliff road, before bearing right onto an unmetalled road that takes you to the Torrs Walk. It is well waymarked. The National Trust have made a further small loop of coastal path just beyond the Tors whereas the official path is signposted inland and over the top of the hill. We suggest you take the National Trust path around Flat Point and Shag Point for preference for the better views it provides, they have no objections if you do.

After this, unfortunately, you come back to the old lane and the Path is taken inland down into Lee so that the fine views you might have had are denied to you. This is doubly disappointing when you realise that some of the property on your right is National Trust but it was an early acquisition and unfortunately no right of access was written into the agreement. There are no refreshments at Lee Bay out of season.

6 | Lee Bay to Woolacombe   OS 180 (V) Lee Bay

Grading: Moderate   Distance –   7   77   5   48

See also our Ilfracombe to Croyde Bay Path Description

This section will take you longer to walk than you think as it includes some up and down work but is a lovely piece of path to walk.

Proceed up the road from Lee, turn right onto a path by the National Trust sign 'Damage Cliff'. To the left of the path are the remains of a pre war golf course. Before Bull Point the path crosses two steep valleys, Hilly Mouth and Bennets Water. The lighthouse is one of the few manned stations left in the country. Rockham has a fine stretch of sands that are very popular in the summer. Morte Point is a spectacular jagged slate ridge rather like a dinosaurs back emerging from the sea. Offshore is the often submerged Morte Stone and this 'Rock of Death' was aptly named in the last century. At certain states of the tide an awesome tidal race can be seen. Many ships have been wrecked off here.

7 | Woolacombe to Croyde Bay   OS 180 (T) Woolacombe

Grading: Moderate   Distance –   8   85   5   53

See also our Ilfracombe to Croyde Bay Path Description

This section starts rather poorly along the road south from Woolacombe and tries hard to lose itself in the enormous dunes. Waymarking, however, has been improved and one should not go astray. A possible alternative is to walk the Marine Drive which gives fine views. If the tide is out it is easier to walk Woolacombe Beach but it should not be attempted on a flood as you may not be able to get off the beach at Vention.

At Vention the hydrangea edged path and then the route through the car park which is unofficial is better than the official route which runs on into the road after the car park. The path climbs up through a field above the cliff to get to the top. It does not go at a lower level.

The high level path out to Baggy Point is pleasant. If the visibility is good you will get a good chance as you turn the corner to look at the path for a number of miles ahead across Bideford Bay. At Baggy Point itself, when you have turned the corner, do swing right on to the lower path. It is no further and provides much better sea views.

8 | Croyde Bay to Barnstaple   OS 180 (V) Croyde

Grading Easy   Distance –   25   110   16   69

See also our Croyde Bay to Appledore Path Description

Distances are measured walking via Crow Point, and around Horsey Island, through Velator to join the disused railway track all the way to Barnstaple.

The path crosses the top of Croyde beach, and onto the low cliffs at Down End, turns left and after reaching the old coast guard lookout, one has to cross the main B3231 road turning left then right to rejoin the path. This then contours Saunton Down End giving some wonderful views across Saunton Beach. The route then crosses the road by the hotel, and after passing round the back of the hotel drops down onto Saunton Sands car park. (Refreshments here in season.)

The official route then crosses the car park, up the approach road onto a track and returns to the B3231 road again.

There is now a walk on this road for about 300 yards with no footpath. Take great care. Take the first turning right after the golf course entrance, through a gate and follow a well way marked track until you reach the main Braunton Burrows National Nature Reserve car park. Turn right and follow a potholed road, which can be very wet in winter, until the Taw estuary comes into sight, here the path forks left. As an alternative one can walk the beach from the Saunton Sands car park, round Airy Point and through the dunes by a cat walk. When you reach the White House turn right and walk the sea wall along the estuary side, past the toll house to reach Velator. Here turn right onto the old railway track, part of the Tarka Trail. It is also a cycle track, and one has a good chance of being run down. This track follows the river all the way to Barnstaple, good walking when the tide is high. Unfortunately there is a bridge missing across a creek, so the path leaves the river side, passing the grandstand of Barnstaple R.F.C. into Mill Road and you are in Barnstaple.

---

9 | Barnstaple to Westard Ho!   OS 180 (T) Barnstaple (B Rail) Instow Appledore

---

Grading Easy   **Distance-**   28   138   17   86

See also our Croyd Bay to Appledore and Appledore to Hartland Point Path Descriptions

Distances are measured walking through to Bideford, 6 miles can be avoided by using the Instow to Appledore Ferry, but this is seasonal and subject to the tide.

The official route through Barnstaple is via High Street, if you do not want to do any shopping, there is a river side walk. After crossing the Rolle bridge aim to walk behind the Civic Centre and the bus station, and you will arrive at the Barnstaple Long Bridge. Cross the River Taw, pass by two mini roundabouts and Shapland yard, and you will see a sign 'Bideford Coast Path', pointing down the road on the right, this then links up with the old railway track. The path then uses this track, again part of the Tarka Trail, and again used by cyclists. Just before you reach the site of the old Yelland power station, turn right and pass the seaward side of the site. At Instow there is the option of using the Ferry.

> Contact Mr Ommanney   April to October 7 days
> The Sea Chest   Three hours either side of high tide
> Market Street
> Appledore EX39 1PW
> Tel: 01237 476191

If the ferry is not running rejoin the old railway track by the old level crossing and signal box.

Continue onto Bideford under the new Bideford bridge, some walkers use this bridge to cross the River Torridge. There is no right of way across this bridge, but it can be walked easily. The old Bideford railway station is the base of the Hartland Coast Heritage Service. Refreshments are available in season in the reconditioned railway carriage.

Cross the Bideford long bridge, turn right and walk along the quay. Continue walking by the river side path now named Landivisau Walk (Bideford's twin town in France) keeping the car park on one's left. At the end of the car park there is a waymarked lane passing the Bideford R.F.C. stadium. Continue walking on a road to pass under the new high level road bridge, then up a rough track, turn right by the way mark, and walk down a narrow track. This rejoins the river side by a small beach at Lower Cleave. There is some more road walking passing the Yeoldon House Hotel. Be sure to keep to the waymarked lane, do not stray up any of the many private drives. After the second war tank traps, fork right and the route enters the N.T. property of Borrough Farm. This is a very pleasant section through some river side woods with fine views back up the river to Bideford.

There is now a steep descent to another small beach with stepping stones over a marshy area. After the second N.T. sign turn right. There are now two options here. A high tide inland diversion has been installed due to a breach in the sea wall but at low tide, continue on along the sea wall. These routes are both well waymarked. With the steps now provided it is not difficult to negotiate the breach in the sea wall. Having done that the path turns inland to meet up with the high tide route. Follow the fence around the Appledore shipyard to reach the road, turn right and follow the waymarked route into Appledore via Myrtle Street.

At Appledore plenty of accommodation and refreshment places are available. Along the Quay we meet the ferry slipway from Instow. The route now continues into old Appledore, passing the homes of the old sailing captains to near the lifeboat house. Due to a cliff fall, there is an inland diversion, but at low tide the beach can be walked passing the ruins of Hinks' boat yard, to reach the road by the entrance of Northern Burrows Country Park. Walk along the side of the road post the D.C.C. recycling centre and out towards the mouth of the Taw/Torridge estuary.

Here for some distance you are walking on the seaward side of the dunes turning to the golf links side to pass Sandy Mere, then it is a straight walk into Westward Ho!. At most states of the tide it is possible to walk the beach, but be warned, the sand can be rather soft in places. Westward Ho! has plenty of accommodation but refreshment places are limited out of season.

10	Westward Ho! to Clovelly	OS 190 (T) Westward Ho!

Grading Strenuous	Distance-	18	156	11	97

See also our Appledore to Hartland Point Path Description

After passing the last of the holiday chalets the path follows the track of the old Bideford to Westward Ho! railway. This is a fine stretch of the coast path over Cornborough and Abbotsham cliffs. At Greencliff a very poor coal was once mined. The path now climbs steeply over Cockington cliffs only to drop again to sea level to cross a pebble beach before climbing again via a wooden staircase, to cross Babbacombe cliffs. At Pepper Combe turn inland to cross the stream and then the path meanders through Sloo woods, to join the new section through Worthygate Wood.

At Bucks Mills refreshments are available. After the climb out of Bucks Mills the path now no longer passes through the holiday village. A new path has been created by the Hartland Heritage coast service. Avoiding the holiday complex completely, the walk along the Hobby Drive is nearly 3 miles long, and takes longer than you think. There is a new path which takes you off the Hobby Drive down to the harbour, and by walking down to it and then up the village street again you can rejoin the coast path.

11	Clovelly to Hartland Quay	OS 190 (V) Clovelly

Grading: Moderate	Distance-	16	172	10	107

See also our Appledore to Hartland Point and Hartland Point to Marsland Mouth Path Descriptions

This is a very fine section indeed. What coastal walking is all about! Allow yourself plenty of time to really enjoy it. Whilst this section is graded moderate overall it could perhaps rate strenuous after Hartland Point.

You leave Clovelly through a large gate which now says 'Please Close All Gates and Keep to Cliff Path'. It is then well signposted for most of the route. you generally follow the fence along until you reach a fourth metal kissing gate which is of double height.

Passing through the tall kissing gate keep on keeping right, you pass an unusual summer house, Angels Wings, but when you reach an arrow pointing left and inland you have a choice. Left is the official and easy path; right are the views and you can always retrace your steps if you do not like the steep path towards the end of the diversion. Following the diversion the first set of steps on the right is a loop with some views, the third set should not be passed without exploration. They lead through a mini tunnel to a surprise view of the sea. You pass another summer house – this time on your left – stone built with a pointed green door and you come out on a platform on the clifftop – another superb view point. From this point a very steep but not dangerous path leads down to rejoin the official path at Mouth Mill. It is very steep – you can always return to the official route if you want.

There is now a good path up through the wood and a stile at the top. The path proceeds through one field and over another stile which is multistepped on the eastern side and then across another field to two stiles: at the right hand one go right, then proceed down the steps, across the bridge at the bottom, turning left, and then take the first turning on the right. This is the more seaward route and is now the official path. We asked for this path and are grateful to the National Trust for having provided it. At Becklands there is a small memorial plaque in memory of the crew of a Wellington bomber that crashed into these cliffs in April 1942.

The route now containues practically on the coast all the way to Eldern Point and then on to Shipload Bay. The true coastal path from Shipload Bay to Barley Bay seaward of the radar station is now open and freely available.

Devon County Council have now stiled and signposted the first stretch from Hartland Point and Titchberry Water, the first stream you come to south of Hartland Point, has been bridged! The path down into the Smoothlands Valley and out to Damehole Point has at least been cleared and if maintenance is kept up, this wonderful part of the coastal path may be as easy on the feet as it is on the eye! Those requiring further exercise may like to walk over the cliff top on the North of the Smoothlands Valley and it does give wonderful views, but it is not the official path. We confidently recommend Damehole Point itself to the sure-footed as not only being one of the most dramatic pieces of definitive right of way in the whole country but also as an ideal picnic spot.

To cross Abbey River the path goes inland behind the cottage to a stone bridge.

After crossing Abbey River, those who want the most scenic route should not turn left as directed at the next coastal path sign. Continue right out to the coast at Dyer's Lookout and then turn left up the cliff edge. It is a little further but scenically much better. Those reaching the Rocket House on the road inland to Stoke and not intending to break their journey may like to be advised that a short distance below them by footpath is the Hartland Quay Hotel which in summer operates a shop, confectionery not grocery! This is a good stopping point for refreshment and accommodation.

| 12 | Hartland Quay to Bude | | | OS 190 (T) Bude | | |

Grading: Severe   Distance-   22   194   14   121

See also our Marsland Mouth to Crackington Haven Path Description

This is a most rewarding but very tough section. It will almost surely take you longer than you think although the beginning is comparatively mild. Before reaching Bude you will have crossed ten river valleys.

The path from Hartland Quay is largely track and becomes a grassy footpath behind St Catherine's Tor. There is then a climb up and down to the waterfall at Speke Mill's Mouth. In our opinion this is the most dramatic waterfall on the whole of the path and we do not forget Pentargon ahead.

The path keeps to the eastern side of the stream for about 150 yards then crosses it by a new wooden footbridge. You pass a footpath sign pointing left and turn left at the second sign 'Coastal Path'. The path now proceeds over Swansford Hill which is a great improvement over the old valley path. Be sure, going up Swansford Hill, to look back at the superb views of St Catherine's Tor, Hartland Quay and Damehole Point. Care should be taken on the section over Milford Common as erosion is making the path extremely narrow and it's a long drop into the sea.

Take care at Sandhole Cliff, after joining the metalled road, to watch for the signpost after about half a mile directing you to turn right to rejoin the coastal path. If you miss this you may find yourself doing about a two-mile walk down the road to Welcombe Mouth. Our Association is urging Devon C.C. to instal a true coast path along Sandhole Cliff.

On the descent into Marsland Mouth look out for a little stone building, once the seaside lookout of the author, Ronald Duncan. It will provide a shelter from the elements.

As you come across the Cornish Border you will start to find a series of extremely helpful and well-thought-out posts. You might smile at the first which says "Cornwall" but thereafter not only do they point the way in each direction, but they also tell you where you are down the shank of the post. Our thanks and appreciation to whoever had this idea – surely the best yet!

The diversion to visit Morwenstow Church is worth consideration. In season refreshments are available at the old rectory. The eccentric Parson Hawker was vicar here in 1830. Look out for his hut which he constructed out of driftwood on Vicarage Cliff.

At Steeple Point there is a tendency to keep too far inland. The official path and the most spectacular one keeps well to seaward. The stream in Combe Valley used to give problems in times of flood, but now, thanks to help from the National Trust and the Countryside Commission's new maintenance scheme, there is a new alternative route with a bridge. In normal times the best proposition is to cross the stream at the mouth across the boulders. By doing so you will miss the chance of refreshments and toilets.

At Sandy Mouth the National Trust have taken over the cafe and improved it. In season it is a welcome refreshment point, but watch the daylight as there is no electricity and the cafe surely closes at darkness at the latest. At Maer Cliff, the official path has fallen into the sea and a diversion has to be made behind the bungalow.

The walking now becomes easier. Soon after Northcott Mouth, Crooklets Beach is reached. Keep to the cliffs passing the cricket pitch. This is the official route and the best way into Bude.

NTG – Page 111 shows incorrect route at Swansford Hill. It goes over the top as waymarked.

| 13 | Bude to Crackington Haven | OS 190 (T) Bude |

| Grading Strenuous | Distance- | 15 | 209 | 9 | 130 |

See also our Marsland Mouth to Crackington Haven Path Description

Bude is quite attractive and has good shops and accommodation, being a fair-sized town. But before you leave do try a short beach walk to the north on the falling tide and look at those cliffs. Alternating bands of sandstone and shale in beautiful curving waves and with eroding continuations of the strata extending out across the beach. This pattern has been with us since Hartland, but as we go south there will soon be a series of changes – from tightly compressed folds to violent crumplings and igneous intrusions of a much more complex nature.

The southbound path starts from the sea lock on the historic Bude Canal, climbs to the cliff top at Compass Point and on to Efford Beacon. Looking back if the tide is out the magnificent beach stretches before you for several miles going absolutely due north, with the dish aerials of the satellite tracking station visible beyond. To the south east if the weather is clear can be seen the high tors of Dartmoor, and to the south west the prominent outline of Cambeak on the south side of the Crackington Haven inlet.

The path over Efford Down and on to Upton is easy enough to follow, and then it is sandwiched between the cliff edge and the road to Widemouth. The beach at Widemouth is popular for swimming and surfing. Toilets, cafes and accommodation are available, but apart from the fine beach with its prominent Black Rock, an unusual stack of slump breccia Widemouth is not attractive. But be prepared, there will be no more facilities until you reach Crackington Haven.

South of Widemouth the path follows the low cliff for a short distance and then diverts inland slightly at Wanson Mouth to join the coast road by the stream valley. Turn west and climb up to Penhalt Cliff. Major subsidence is occurring and the coast path has long gone, but don't blame the County Council, you will see that the road is going as well! At the southern end of the clifftop car park the coast path proper recommences through a field and then descends steeply into Millook Haven. Those with a geological interest should go on to the stony beach to view the remarkable chevron folded rock strata in the cliff on the north side – a classic textbook photograph and in sharp contrast to the curving folds to the north beyond Widemouth.

Follow the steep road beyond the stream crossing in Millook for a short distance then branch right on to the cliff top path at Ravens Beak. From here the path climbs steadily but is fairly easy going all the way to Chipman Point. Note the ancient stunted oak wood in the area of Dizzard Point. The stream valley at Chipman Point is steep and deep, one of a series ahead, some with spectacular waterfalls cascading over into the rocky beach below. A tough ascent, then a further drop into the valley at Cleave Strand followed by a ridge walk at Castle Point giving tremendous views. The descent to the Coxford Water stream is severe and the climb onwards to Pencarrow Point will certainly exercise the heart lung system. Pause to recover and enjoy the views before the descent into Crackington Haven.

CP – Dizzard Point – The path is nearer the coast then the map suggests. The variant – Fire Beacon Point to Pentargon is now the official route.

NTG – Page 122 last sentence. You have another steep up and down at Aller Shoot.

BMG – Page 22. Path just south of Wanson Mouth is on the road.

| **Grading: Strenuous** | | **Distance-** | 12 | 221 | 7 | 137 |

See also our Crackington Haven to Tintagel Path Description

At Crackington Haven it is usually safe for a swim, but never go out of your depth on Cornwall's north coast. There are toilets and a seasonal shop, pub and cafe, and a long, tough, remote stretch path ahead. Again, the folds in the rock strata are remarkable, with interesting patterns down on the beach at Tremoutha Haven. Take particular care at Cambeak, the cliff edge all round is terrifying, but just look at the view. Hartland and Lundy Island to the north; Tintagel and Rumps Point to the south.

The path is now relatively level and generally stays above the massive landslip zone at Strangles Beach. There is a good path down through the landslip to the beach, which is interesting and pleasant at low tide, but it is an arduous climb back. At the northern end of the beach is the conspicuous Northern Door rock arch. There is access to the road and car parking at the National Trust Trevigue Farm.

Ahead looms High Cliff, the highest point on the coast path in Cornwall and best avoided when a gale is blowing. Just before High Cliff the path goes round the back of a small stream valley where there is a diversity of minor paths, but then just aim for the top. The southbound descent from High Cliff is precipitously steep so take it slowly, then the path up through the massive landfall at Rusey Cliff twists and turns through the brambles and gorse. This is a major geological fault zone. The path is easier to follow than it used to be, but the ground here is soily and the vegetation grows rampantly in summer which presents a continuing problem to the County Council who have difficulty keeping it cleared back.

Once at the top of Rusey Cliff there follows an easier stretch through grassy sheep fields, with the approach to Buckator now being more coastal than shown in earlier guides.

The sheer black cliff of Buckator hangs over the sea inlet, with impressive white bands of quartz running through, quite different from the folded and predominantly sandstone rocks to the north. The path dips slightly to cross a marshy stream where stepping stones provide firm footing, then continues on at high level to Fire Beacon Point. Here the descent is steep but there are attractive slate steps on the most precipitous part. The path then keeps close to the cliff edge and into the Pentargon inlet where an impressive waterfall cascades down to the sea. The best view of this is now from the southern side, cliff falls having caused the path on the north side to be diverted and the old viewpoint has been lost.

Further cliff falls seem imminent on the south side of Pentargon, but from here on it is easy going into Boscastle. Aim for the white mast atop Penally Hill, or take a short cut left just before. Either way you find yourself walking alongside the beautiful harbour inlet and past the Youth Hostel into the village of Boscastle. Penally Point is well worth the detour, an exciting viewpoint, but the slaty rock is dangerously slippery when wet. Note the extraordinary small scale distortions in the strata alongside the path.

NTG – Pages 125 and 127. Show incorrect route at Buckator. Follow the field edge around.

| **Grading: Moderate** | | **Distance-** | 8 | 229 | 5 | 142 |

See also our Crackington Haven to Tintagel Path Description

There are shops, pubs, toilets, accommodation and an excellent Heritage Coast Centre in Boscastle, and the old village up the lane by the Wellington Hotel is well worth exploring.

The next section on to Tintagel is shorter and easier then the two previous sections. The path leaves from the south side of the harbour and climbs steeply past the gully to Eastern Blackapit to the Willapark headland with its prominent white watch tower. Go up to the watch tower, or take the short cut across the back of the headland past the ancient Forrabury strip field system now preserved by The National Trust. The path soon descends into the stream valley of Grower Gut – there are some granite stepping stones to help you if the water is in flood. Further on the path turns sharp right to keep to the seaward side of the Manor House and onto a prominent headland which overlooks Short Island. If you are a birdwatcher here is a good place to stop, picnic and observe through binoculars. Both Short Island and its neighbour Long Island are densely populated with breeding seabirds during the early summer, including Guillemots, Razor-bills and a few Puffins. Always look down on the water, they tend to float around in groups when off duty.

As you go on past Firebeacon Hill look for the Ladies Window rock arch in the gully to the right. From here to Rocky Valley the going is level, but do look back to the dramatic pinnacles below Trevalga Cliff. Soon on your left you are confronted by a conspicuous cliff top caravan/camp site, but perhaps you are planning to stay there! Trewethet Gut is a dangerous and eroding inlet that has necessitated a slight diversion of the path, and then you descend into the exquisite Rocky Valley. Look for seals in the surging sea as you cross the footbridge, and for the Dippers that feed in the water of the stream. There is a path through Rocky Valley to the coast road, where cars may be parked.

From the footbridge a steep climb to high level again, and you find yourself overlooking Bossiney Haven. There is a cross-road of paths giving access to the beach from Bossinney village, and indeed this is an excellent place for a swim just after low tide. But the coast path goes on straight ahead and bears right to another prominent headland called Willapark, the second in just two miles. Again birdwatchers should go to the end and scan The Sisters and the ocean through binoculars. There are often Terns, Gannets and even Shearwaters further out. But beware the precipitous cliff edge as you return to the path. Then on to Barras Nose headland, dominated by that awful hotel eyesore, and down to Tintagel Haven below the Castle ruins. Here there are toilets and a cafe.

---

16 | Tintagel to Port Isaac　　　　　　　　　　　　　　OS 200 (T) Tintagel

Grading: Severe　　　　　　　　　　　　Distance-　　13　　242　　8　　150

See also our Tintagel to Port Isaac Path Description

Tintagel has many shops, cafes and guest houses. It is not attractive like the fishing ports of Port Isaac and Padstow that lie ahead, but the Old Post Office, owned and restored by the National Trust, dates back to the fourteenth century when it was no doubt a house of some importance.

Around The Island and down in Tintagel Haven there is some interesting and complex geology with older rocks (Devonian) overthrusted on top of more recent rocks (carboniferous), and bands of Lava and Tuff. The severe erosion, which is no doubt compounded by these faults and thrusts, is making access to The Island increasingly difficult to maintain. In the shelter of Tintagel Haven sailing ships used to be loaded with the high quality slate that is still extracted from several quarries inland away from this highly disturbed coastal zone.

The path to Trebarwith Strand climbs up from Tintagel Haven below and to the left of the Castle entrance and gives an excellent view of the upside down rocks on the south face of The Island. From here on and past St Materiana's Church it is easy going. The Youth Hostel at Dunderhole Point was once a quarry office building. The National Trust are endeavouring to tidy up the cliff top here which has been severely scarred by uncontrolled motor vehicle access. There are further old quarries ahead as you approach Hole Beach and Trebarwith Strand, and surprisingly sailing ships were loaded under the cliffs at Penhallic Point where the remains of the wharf can still be seen. The path drops down by the toilets in Trebarwith Strand, and opposite is a welcome pub serving hot food. The beach is worth exploring at low tide, but watch that you don't get cut off, and do be warned that swimming can be dangerous here.

From here to Port Isaac the path is long and in parts very tough. The descents to the valley streams and up again on the other side are about the steepest on the whole of the South West Way. Do not leave Trebarwith Strand unless you have food, energy and plenty of time in hand. The climb up out of Trebarwith Strand, which is stepped almost all the way, will give you a foretaste of what lies ahead. And having reached the top, you must go all the way down again into Backways Cove, then up again to a more restful level stretch for about one mile to the stream valley behind Tregardock Beach where you are confronted by a detached and eroding piece of the cliff known as The Mountain. As you descend on the inland side of The Mountain you will meet a cross-roads of paths from Tregardock village to the beach., The beach is worth a visit at low tide but your route lies straight ahead and you have quite a long way to go.

From here the stretch marked on the maps as Tregardock Cliff is easy enough, but at Jacket's Point the deepest and steepest valley of all lies before you, the commencement of The

National Trust Dannonchapel property. An excellent job has been done on the path, the stream crossing and the staircase of steps on the ascent on the south side. But having reached the top, just past the ugly wartime lookout you drop down again into yet another deep valley. A short diversion out to the cliff edge just before you make the descent reveals a dramatic and dangerous rocky scene with a mineworking tunnel cut through from the valley side. More steps up on the south side of the valley, then over to the Barretts Zawn stream valley where another mineworking adit faces you. This gave donkey access to the Barretts Zawn beach – our advice is don't try it.

On the climb up round the Barretts Zawn cliffs you will certainly see that there have been massive rock falls and that another will occur any time. Then you descend very steeply on the south side into the next stream valley at Ranie Point, and as you slide down the stony slope you may well feel that the path here could be improved. Some walkers evidently complain about the staircases of steps on these valley sides, but they are so exceptionally steep we believe that steps are the best option and we have been urging the hard-pressed County Council to put some here.

Now at last the path levels out through the sheep meadows with just a small valley to cross at St Illickswell Gug where a board walk takes you across the marsh. When you reach the road at Cartway Cove the official path is directly opposite and drops down by the side of the hotel at Portgaverne. But if you still have energy take the path to the right and go round The National Trust headland and if the tide is out walk along the old harbour quay where sailing ships were once loaded with slate. Either way there is then a short road walk up to the cliff car park at Port Isaac. Go through this past the public toilets and follow the well signed path round to overlook the attractive inlet and hence the village street. Cornwall Heritage Coast Service has an information centre at the Old School Hotel, Port Isaac. Tel: Bodmin (01208) 880721.

17	**Port Isaac to Polzeath**			**OS 200 (V) Port Isaac**

Grading: Strenuous		Distance-	14	256	9	159

See also our Port Isaac to Padstow Path Description

Port Isaac is a gem, with narrow streets and tiny cottages which are no doubt easier to look at than to live in. There are two excellent pubs and one of the cafes is in an extremely old and crooked little building. Do take time to explore the back streets and the small fish market, and see if you can find Squeezibelly Alley!

Another tough walk lies ahead and there are no facilities until you reach Polzeath, but the scenery is superb. Take the road to the right behind the fish market and past more toilets. The path bears right along the cliff in front of two prominent guest houses and takes you on past Lobber Point then down into Pine Haven. From here on the path is relatively new and apart from an unpleasant fenced corridor cutting off Varley Head, it really is magnificent, and keeps close to the cliff edge all the way to Portquin. The fence stays on your left for over a mile of steep ups and downs, but it does protect you from the enormous herd of beef cattle that generally roam the meadows behind during the summer. Watch out for the Peregrines that hunt along this stretch and for the occasional adder basking in the sun quite close to the path!

At Kellan Head The Rumps promontory faces you at the far end of Portquin Bay. Then as you turn the corner the path overlooks the beautiful Port Quin inlet and descends to the village, once a busy little pilchard port, but there are no facilities here now. Follow the road westbound until half way up the steep hill where a new slate stile gives access to the south side of the inlet. You are on National Trust land and free to explore Doyden Point, formed from rocks of pillow lava, but we shall see more of this shortly. The new path follows the stream valley some distance in front of the old Prison Governor's House, and soon passes two fenced mineshafts where you might still find interesting mineral samples amongst the loose spoil material nearby – but keep away from the dangerous cliff edge!

At Trevan Point there is a sharp descent to Epphaven Cove which with its neighbour Lundy Bay has a beautiful beach at low tide. You then enter a surprisingly wooded valley where in late spring you will hear the delightful call of the Willow Warbler. As you climb up out of the bay look out for the startling Lundy Hole behind a protective fence on your right. On the cliff top again as you approach The Rumps you will see the earth ramparts of an Iron Age Fort in the lower ground in front of the headland. When you get there the detour through the entrance and on round the rocks over-looking The Mouls island is well worthwhile and can give good seabird watching.

Then quite easy going on to Pentire Point, another headland formed from pillow lava. A perfect cross-section can be seen in the small vertical rock face on your left as you leave The Rumps headland, the rounded hollow shapes having been formed by viscous rolling of the molten lava under the sea. The walling stone alongside the path reveals the structure of small holes in the rock caused by gases and steam, but do not remove pieces as samples, The National Trust spend much time and money maintaining these walls and they provide wind shelter for the sheep.

There are many good viewpoints on the South West Way, but that from Pentire Point is one of the best. In clear conditions south to Trevose Head and beyond, and north to Bude, the satellite tracking station and even Hartland Quay and Lundy Island, but you will need binoculars! Then follows an easy descent into Polzeath with the Camel Estuary before you and Stepper Point with its Daymark Tower on the opposite side. In contrast to the last 20 miles of perfection, the cliff top housing and car parking in New and Old Polzeath are unfortunate, but the sea, the sand and the surf are magnificent. There are toilets on the left as you reach the road beyond Pentireglaze Haven. The path continues along the cliff edge to the village centre and gives access to the beach on the way. And yes, there are ice cream vans on the beach, go and have one, they are excellent.

18	Polzeath to Padstow	OS 200 (V) Polzeath (V) Rock

Grading: Easy	Distance-	5	261	3	162

See also our Port Isaac to Padstow Path Description

Polzeath is a surfers' paradise with several shops, cafes, accommodation and campsites. On the left by the park is a small Tourist Information Office and there are toilets opposite.

Follow the road past the beach car park and take the path right by the cottages where the road bends sharp left on the steep hill. The path follows the edge of Tristram Cliff where you can watch the expertise of the surfers. From here to Daymer Bay the path along The Greenaway is intensively walked throughout the year and measures have had to be taken to discourage people from wandering off the route and scarring the fragile turf with alternative tracks. In fact the newly laid path is so good it is now classed as suitable for the disabled in wheelchairs, which is almost unique on the South West Way. There are houses on your left, but the coastal scene is beautiful with a rocky sea washed platform below, the haunt of Curlews, Redshanks, Grey Plover and Oystercatchers, and the headlands of Stepper Point and Pentire Point in the background. Many fishing and pleasure boats can be observed entering and leaving from Padstow some two miles up the Camel Estuary.

Just off Trebetherick Point is the Doom Bar, noticeable only at low tide when the waves are breaking over the sand. There were many wrecks here during the days of sail when ships were largely at the mercy of wind and tide. The rusted remains of a capstan used for winching sailing ships in over the bar can be seen on the rocks below the path, and there were others across at Stepper Point. Alongside the path near Trebetherick Point are the hardened remains of an older beach which is now about 25 feet above the present high water line. And on rare occasions in Daymer Bay during the winter the sea scours out the sand to reveal preserved tree stumps and roots in a bed of peat. There was woodland here some 4,000 years ago when the sea level was lower. All to do with global warming and cooling and the amount of ice at the poles! There are toilets and a cafe in Daymer Bay car park and the beach is one of the safest for a swim – but keep out of the estuary channel at low tide.

The coast path goes down the steps on to the beach and then through the dunes and over a footbridge just below Brea Hill. To visit little St Enodoc Church which was once buried beneath the blown sand, turn left midway along the dunes and follow the white markers across the Golf Course. You must then retrace your route back to the dunes, or you can go on through the Golf Course to rejoin the coast path in the dunes on the far side of Brea Hill, but this is a busy Golf Course and you may wish you had a protective helmet and visor. Your route through the Golf Course is marked by large white painted rocks. From the footbridge you can go either way round Brea Hill, or straight over the top! Alternatively, if the tide is out you can walk along the beach to Rock and the Padstow ferry. All routes are pleasant and the sheltered estuary surroundings make quite a change from the exposed cliffs that you have been used to. The official path goes through a hollow just behind the dunes on the south side of Brea Hill, a Site of Special Scientific Interest for the rare plant life that thrives on the calcium rich sand. At the southern end the path branches left to a higher level and on to Rock car park, but you can continue on along the beach except at very high tide. There are toilets in the car park and the ferry landing is on the shore below. Be warned however that at exceptionally low tides the ferry may sail from quite some distance downstream in front of the dunes, so keep a lookout as you walk.

Rock/Padstow (River Camel)
Black Tor Ferry
Padstow Harbour Commissioners,
Harbour Office, West Quay,
Padstow, Cornwall PL28 8AQ.
Tel: Padstow (01841) 532239
Fax: (01841) 533346

Ferry operates all year, except Sundays from November to first Sunday in April (unless Easter is early) at intervals of 10/15 minutes. Times 0750 hrs to 1650 hrs. Last ferry times are extended to 1950 hrs in the summer according to demand. The last ferry – Rock to Padstow is 20 minutes earlier than 1650 and 1950. There may be a reduction in service during the middle of the day in winter but ferry will run if required, weather permitting.

We understand that this ferry company are no longer keen to issue single fares but we have been told that they will do so for genuine walkers on request and accordingly you should ask for a single fare if that is what you require.

19   Padstow to Trevone   OS 200 (T) Padstow

Grading: Easy   Distance-   8   269   5   167

See also our Padstow to Porthcothan Path Description

Normally the Padstow ferry will take you into the harbour, but at low tide it will deposit you a short distance downstream at St Saviour's Point, just below the path to Stepper Point. Do not take this as an opportunity to cut out Padstow, you must go into the town and explore. The harbour area, the narrow lanes in the old town and up to St Petroc's Church are attractive and fairly traffic free. A glass of beer and a genuine Cornish steak pasty make an excellent traditional lunch. A visit to the Tourist Information Centre on the harbour is recommended, and on your way it is interesting to look at the places of origin of the many fishing boats – all ports from the Hebrides to the Channel Islands!

The coast path starts on your left at the north end of the harbour and is wide and well trodden. In the early summer Blackcaps and Warblers sing in the wooded stream valley at St George's Cove. From Gun Point you can, if the tide is out, take a short cut across the beach to Hawker's Cove by the prominent old Lifeboat House. If the tide is in you can enjoy a quiet swim, this is a very pleasant and usually wind sheltered beach. Round the back of the old pilots' houses from Hawker's Cove and then a climb up to Stepper Point with its disused Coastguard Lookout and the stone built Daymark Tower. From this high ground there is a remarkable panorama behind you and on a clear day you will see the granite tors of Bodmin Moor in the distance.

So now we are back on the exposed Atlantic Coast. Approaching the precipitous inlet of Butter Hole Cove look out for the small Pepper Hole a few yards to the right of the path. There follows a long easy stretch to Gunver Head followed by a steep descent to the small stream valley. The rocky pinnacles of the Merope Islands just behind you are spectacular. A short climb up again and soon you will see ahead the marble cliff of Porthmissen Bridge. This comprises many bands of hard limestone and softer shale on which Razorbills and Guillemots nest in the summer. At Roundhole Point the path skirts the impressive Round Hole collapsed cave which should be approached with caution, and then descends to the car park at Trevone.

20   Trevone to Porthcothan   OS 200

Grading: Easy   Distance-   12   281   7   174

See also our Padstow to Porthcothan Path Description

There are toilets, a cafe and a good beach in Trevone, but little else of interest to the walker except perhaps some bed and breakfast accommodation. The path passes behind the little headland on the south side of the bay and follows the cliff edge round rocky Newtrain Bay. There has been a cliff collapse here causing the path to be re-routed round, but then it returns to the cliff edge and on to St Cadoc's Point and Harlyn Bay. Here again there are refreshments, toilets and a beautiful beach.

33

The stream generally has to be crossed via the road bridge, and then the path follows the beach for about 300 metres before climbing slightly into the dunes and so on past the end of the bay to Cataclews Point. The hard erosion resistant dolerite rock here was used to make the polished font in Padstow Church. In Mother Ivey's Bay there are some unpleasant man-made features which mar the coastal scene, including an often foul smelling sewage discharge which frequently contaminates the nearby beaches. There is a huge and conspicuous caravan site near Trevose Farm, and access to the headland by the new Padstow Lifeboat Station is barred by an ugly concrete and mesh fence reminiscent of prison camps which is in sharp contrast to the old Tamarisk hedges nearby. How sadly all this compares with the painstaking remedial and conservation work that has been carried out by The National Trust on long stretches of the coast to the north of the Camel Estuary.

At Trevose Head you can generally visit the immaculately kept lighthouse, but keep away when the fog horn is blowing! On a clear day you will see the granite hills of West Penwith behind St Ives to the south and the satellite tracking dish aerials beyond Bude to the north. Turning south, the path passes yet another large Round Hole as it descends to Booby's Bay. There is something of a rocky scramble to get through to Constantine Bay, but it is beautiful here with a particularly attractive beach at low tide. Not really safe for swimming unfortunately. Beyond the dunes the path leaves the beach to go round Treyarnon Point, revealing another attractive beach at Treyarnon Bay. The Youth Hostel is on the left, and in the car park area there are toilets and refreshments. If you are intent on swimming, observe the safety notices which will certainly tell you not to do so at low tide.

An unusually indented coastline follows beyond Trethias Island, but the path cuts across the narrower headlands. Between Pepper Cove and Warren Cove are the ramparts of an Iron Age Fort, and in Fox Cove you may see the remains of a ship which ran aground in 1969. Minnows Islands and the cove beyond are quite spectacular, then the path turns into Porthcothan Bay, descending through the protected National Trust strip which contrasts with the housing development on the side opposite.

21 | Porthcothan to Newquay OS 200

Grading: Moderate Distance- 15 296 10 184

See also our Porthcothan to Newquay Path Description

Porthcothan has toilets, a shop and limited accommodation. The path leaves past the shop and keeps in front of the houses and on round the headland overlooking Trescore Islands. There is a steep descent into Porth Mear valley, a popular spot for birdwatchers, and an equally steep climb up again, then an easy walk to Park Head, another spectacular viewpoint. Ahead lies the famous Bedruthan Steps property of the National Trust, with a beautiful beach at low tide. As you leave Park Head you will see that the cliff is slowly sliding down, although it has been like this for many years. The beach itself has a recurring accessibility problem due to the dangerous condition of the cliffs, but a great deal of money is being spent on the long flight of steps down. If the tide is on its way out it is worth going down to explore the rock stacks, but don't get cut off and don't even think about swimming. The National Trust cafe and Information Centre in the car park are open throughout the summer.

Bedruthan Steps can be a busy place, but few people stray far from their cars and you will soon find yourself on a quieter stretch of path to Trenance Point. A steady descent into Mawgan Porth follows, where the road must be used for a short distance in order to cross the stream. There are toilets and shops here. The southbound path leaves to the right on the sharp road bend on the hill out of Mawgan Porth. Then follows a long high level stretch to Watergate Bay, with minor descents at Beacon Cove and Stem Cove, between which across Griffin's Point headland are the ramparts of another Iron Age Fort. Just inland is the airport and RAF station at St Mawgan, and you may find yourself being targeted by high powered military jet aircraft as they come in to land. Ahead lies the magnificent Watergate Beach, but the path remains at high level until it crosses to the road behind the Watergate Hotel.

After crossing the stream bridge by the car park, where there are toilets, the path leaves to the right from the road to Newquay and again climbs to the high clifftop where it remains all the way to Whipsiderry. Here some ugly clifftop development has been permitted, but the coastal scene is great, with Newquay and Towan Head in the background. The cliffs at Whipsiderry are high and precipitous, but there are steps down to the beach and some caves to explore. The path just manages to squeeze between a guesthouse and the cliff edge, and then takes you on to Trevelgue

Head. We recommend that you cross the footbridge on to the island, where a rough sea can be most spectacular. Then you must return to the road at Porth Beach where there are toilets and cafes. You may then walk out along the southern edge of the beach rather than taking the official road route, joining the path by more toilets. From here it crosses the headland between Porth and Lusty Glaze, an hotel having claimed the old path round the headland. This short cut avoids the road and takes you round the cliff edge at Lusty Glaze Cove and into the Barrowfields Park. Then you are on the road into Newquay town centre, but if the tide is out you can walk along the magnificent beach from Lusty Glaze or from Barrowfields all the way to the harbour. The Youth Hostel is across the road from Barrowfields.

BMG – Does not cover total mileage through Newquay.

| 22 | Newquay to Holywell | OS 200 (T) Newquay (B.Rail) (V) Crantock |

Grading: Moderate   Distance-   8   302   5   189

See also our Newquay to Perranporth Path Description

Newquay is the biggest town on the north coast and the pedestrianised shopping centre is quite attractive. There is no shortage of restaurants, pubs and accommodation here, and there is even a railway station! But do explore the beaches and the harbour before you leave, and if the tide is out you can gain access to the coast path by the steps at the back of the harbour.

The path leaves just above the harbour and climbs past the old Huer's Hut to Towan Head. In the cliffs below the Hut is a noisy Kittiwake colony, and this is a very good spot to observe the differences between Kittiwakes, Fulmars, Black-headed Gulls and the rest. Towan Head is particularly good for seabird watching, with binoculars you may spot Gannets, Petrels and Shearwaters further out.

From Towan Head the path follows along the back of Fistral Beach. This is probably the most popular surfing beach in the British Isles, international competitions are held here. The path climbs to the cliffs at the southern end, passing in front of the housing development at Pentire, then across the headland at The Warren over to The Gannel river estuary. The proprietors of the Fern Pit Cafe on Riverside Crescent operate a summer season only ferry service to Crantock Beach, supplemented by a low tide portable footwalk. In the winter months the County Council recommend their official crossing about half a mile upstream via the tidal bridge to Penpol Creek. This may not be usable for up to 2½ hours before and after high tide, so we strongly recommend that you study the tide tables in Newquay and time your departure accordingly, but in the summer there is a ferry service here also.

Newquay/Crantock (River Gannel)
Fern Pit Cafe and Ferry
Proprietor – G.A. Northey
Fern Pit, Riverside Crescent, Newquay TR7 1PJ
Tel: Crantock (01737) 873181

End of May to mid September
1000–1800
Continuous 7 day week.

Newquay/Penpol Creek (River Gannel)
L.P. Crantock, St Christopher, Vosporth Road,
Crantock, Newquay, Cornwall.
Tel: Crantock (01637) 830478

Seasonal. Late Spring Bank Holiday
to mid September. Continuous during
tide (weather permitting).

You will be able to see the Penpol footwalk from the road at the Fern Pit Cafe. If the Fern Pit facilities are closed, continue east along Riverside Crescent and Riverside Avenue, passing Fistral Crescent into Pentire Crescent where the public footpath to Crantock is signposted right. This leads down to the river bank and the footwalk is ahead of you. Cross over the river on to the sands and aim for the low cliff on your right at the outlet of Penpol Creek. Here there are rough steps cut in the slaty rock up to the public footpath along the south bank of the Gannel which takes you to Crantock Beach. If you study the map you will see that a short cut can be taken from the Fistral coast path where it climbs on to the Pentire cliffs. Go left along Pentire Crescent just beyond the toilets and straight over to the signposted Crantock footpath.

Another route from Newquay town centre is via Tregunnel Hill to the Trenance footbridge just downstream from the boating lake across the new A3075 road extension. This is not usable for about 1 hour before and after high tide and involves a long walk via Trevemper and Treringey into Penpol Creek.

Crantock Beach is attractive at low tide and can give good views of terns fishing in The Gannel below the cliffs of Pentire Point East. The path passes behind the dunes to the National Trust car park at Rushy Green, then westwards through the dunes to the cliffs of Pentire Point West. Alternatively you may walk along the beach to gain access to the path by scrambling up at the western end of the dunes.

Porth Joke is a sheltered sandy inlet, then follows a climb to Kelsey Head, another Iron Age site. From here in the distance can be seen St Agnes Head with Bawden Rocks offshore. Holywell Beach lies before you and the path descends to the dunes and hence into Holywell, but you may prefer to go on to the beach and to explore the rocks at its southern end. It is not necessary to enter the village, the stream can usually be crossed to gain access to the path which climbs over to Penhale Point.

NTG – Page 35. First line – You can only use that bridge when the cafe is open.

23	Holywell to Perranporth	OS 200

Grading: Moderate, but if the tide is close in and one has to use the sand dune route to get to Perranporth, it certainly becomes strenuous.

Distances-	10	314	6	195

See also our Newquay to Perranporth Path Description

The path cuts across Penhale Point headland and then skirts the seaward edge of the rather ugly Penhale Camp where there is a short fenced section. The army presence here however has served to preserve the beautiful wild dunes area inland from being overrun by campsites and chalets, and it now deserves to be protected as a nature reserve. Then out to Ligger Point and the first good view of the long Perran Beach. As the path takes you towards the dunes you will see the rusty coloured Perran Iron Lode in the cliff quarry. The path descends behind this and follows the back of the beach for almost a mile then climbs up through the dunes behind the rock cliff at Cotty's Point. The incoming tide will reach the foot of the cliff here but there are escape steps to the dunes at each side and if the tide is out you can continue on along the beach rather than going over the top. The path descends to the back of the beach just south of Cotty's Point, crosses the stream by a footbridge and so takes you into the town or the car park where there are toilets.

24	Perranporth to St Agnes	OS 204 (T) Perranporth

Grading: Moderate	Distance-	6	320	4	199

See also our Perranporth to Portreath Path Description

Perranporth is a busy holiday centre during the summer and has good shops and accommodation. The eroding rock stacks at the southern end of the beach are interesting, and may be explored using the beach access at the far end of the car park in front of the hotel terrace. Round the corner you will find a staircase from the beach up to the cliff car park at Droskyn Point. The official route leaves west from the town car park and follows the hill up Cliff Road, but just to the left of the Atlantic House Hotel there are some steps up and a footpath which takes you past the Droskyn Point car park. Whichever way you have chosen, keep inland of the prominent castellated building and on along Tregundy Lane to the end of the houses. The southbound coast path is signposted half left at the entrance drive to the Youth Hostel and the new South West Water sewage pumping station. It then descends slightly to the right before climbing to the cliffs overlooking Shag rock.

From here on you will see increasing evidence of mining activity. The path is fairly level going, passing the small outcrop of granite at Cligga Head which has been quarried and displays conspicuous stripes of greisen (for the chemistry of which you must consult the textbooks!). The mineralisation along the coast here and to the south is attributable to the intrusion of the granite which extends over a considerable area below the surface. Southbound through the quarry and mineworkings you are unlikely to lose the path. Hanover Cove is named after a shipwreck. The rock formations around the cove are dramatic and green copper stains the cliffs. There are many mineshafts hereabouts capped with conical steel mesh which allows access for bats.

The long stretch to Trevallas Porth is level easy going alongside the airfield perimeter, you will progress much faster here than you did further north. There is a sharp descent into Trevellas Coombe where there are many mine workings with their decaying buildings. Go upstream to the bridge which crosses the stream in front of the Blue Hills engine house and then half right over the top to Trevaunance Cove. The path passes perilously close to the precipitous cliff edge, but there is another track slightly further back. Past the waste tips and the capped mineshafts still at high level the path forks, left direct to St Agnes avoiding the road and right down to the road at Trevaunance Cove. Cross over the road and turn right behind the four storey grey rendered housing block and the official path takes you past the toilets. If you go down into the cove where there is a seasonal cafe, there is a footpath behind the Jubilee Terrace and steps back up to the path near the Trevaunance Point Hotel. This has a pleasant garden where you can enjoy the view and a glass of beer.

It is possible to cross the beach from Trevallas Porth to Trevaunance Cove at low tide, but be warned that the boulders are dangerously slippery. Surprisingly there was once a harbour under the cliff on the west side of Trevaunance Cove, but all you will find now is a tumbled mass of granite blocks.

BMG – Path loops inland at Trevellas Porth.

25	St Agnes to Porthtowan			OS 203 (V) St Agnes		
Grading: Moderate		Distance-	8	328	5	204

See also our Perranporth to Portreath Path Description

Beyond the Trevaunance Point Hotel the path climbs left past some unusual mine workings. From the top it stays at high level out to St Agnes Head, passing many mineshafts and waste tips on the way. Here you are circumnavigating St Agnes Beacon, a small outcrop of granite half a mile back from the coast. As the path turns south you will see Godrevy Lighthouse across the bay, with St Ives and the massive granite of Penwith beyond. The going is relatively easy and soon you will pass the much photographed Towanroath Engine House, part of the Wheal Coates tin and copper mine and now preserved by The National Trust. The path then descends into Chapel Porth where there is a car park, toilets and a seasonal cafe. At low tide if you walk some distance north along the beach you will see a streak of copper ore in the cliff beneath the Towanroath shaft.

The southbound path climbs steeply out of Chapel Porth past more mineshafts and waste tips on Mulgram Hill, then follows a good clifftop walk to Porthtowan. The path descends to the back of the beach and on past the car park where there are toilets. The transition from mining to tourism here has produced some unattractive features but the beach is beautiful and extensive at low tide, from Tobban Horse in the south to Chapel Porth in the north.

BMG – Path loops inland at Porthtowan.

26	Porthtowan to Portreath			OS 203 (V) Porthtowan		
Grading: Strenuous		Distance-	6	334	4	208

See also our Perranporth to Portreath Path Description

Porthtowan is popular for surfing and has accommodation and a few shops and seasonal cafes. To find the southbound path turn right along West Beach Road then left up the narrow road to the cliff top. You will see a steep path up from the west beach, but parts of this seem to be in imminent danger of slipping away so we cannot recommend it. On the headland the path turns south, passing many mineworkings, and keeps some distance back from the crumbling and dangerous cliff edge. At the steep valley drop to Sally's Bottom steps have been installed on either side, then on reaching high level again you find yourself walking alongside the unattractive Nancekuke fence which encloses the large military establishment just inland. You may not be convinced, but the new fence is lower and less intimidating than the one it replaces. It stays with us for over a mile and almost to Portreath, where the Daymark above the harbour entrance can be seen ahead. The path turns south just before you reach the Daymark, avoiding another dangerous cliff edge, and joins the road down to the harbour. The long narrow inlet is unusual, but the protective pier which extends over the rocks on the south side is now out of bounds, too many people have been swept off by waves breaking over.

Grading: Strenuous in parts   Distance-   19   353   12   220

See also our Portreath to Hayle Path Description

There are shops, cafes and bed and breakfast accommodation in Portreath, but the beach is small in comparison with most on this coast. To gain the southbound path go round the harbour to the beach car park then to the right up Battery Hill. Where this road drops to the beach again at the western end, the coast path branches left up the valley to the clifftop. The surface can be wet and muddy, it is far better to climb to the right by the National Trust sign and go over Western Hill, this path continues through to join the coast path overlooking Western Cove.

You soon enter Western Hill N.T. property where there is a choice; the old official route is forward and misses out the fine views from Western Hill and the possibility of seeing seals out by Gull Rock. There is already a minor path going right and the N.T. have promised to improve this and we then hope it will become the new official route, it always should have been.

At Bassett's Cove you go through a big car park and start several miles of easy cliff top walking. There are practically no signs but only two places you are likely to go astray. For a mile and a half you get closer to the road and then start to get away from it again; after a further half mile you should observe a small field ahead and to your left, here you have to fork right and then turn right.

You pass Hell's Mouth which has a seasonal cafe just across the road, then when you are approaching another field you come out on to a track where you turn right *but* this time do not take the next right as it is a beach path only. We have asked N.T. for signing in both these places.

There is then a very pleasant walk around Navax and Godrevy Points, there are good views out to sea, ahead to St Ives and what to many is a surprise southwards. You then have to negotiate a big car park but by keeping well to seaward you can miss most of it and the road that leads to it.

At Magow Rocks if the tide is out it is decision time again. Tide out, scramble down over Magow Rocks, wade across Red River, so called because it once was really red, walk along the sands. If the tide is right out you can go round the corner at Black Head and pick up the route again from the estuary going into Hayle. More often you have to go up on the cliffs towards the end of the beach, look for caravans behind and an old war time blockhouse in front. It is a hard climb up the soft sand but this is better option than the 'tide in' route!

Tide in, follow the road from a cafe, it briefly becomes a track again, turn right at main road B3201 and follow that until you have passed first bungalow on right. There opposite 'Gwithian' sign is the path you want.

You now have a 'spot the post' competition amongst the dunes. There is certainly no logic in the route and unless it is cowslip time you will be regretting the tide was in. We think that most who attempt the dunes survive, but as we get no complaints from those who don't, we can not really be sure!

The route becomes beset by caravans and chalets and, eventually when you have given up all hope, arrives in a big open car park area. Go out the other end and down a broad track. Here swing right in front of Hayle Bulk Supply Point; if you think the area is grotty take comfort from the fact it was once worse, they had a coal fired power station here! Go ahead to cross the bridge to swing right into Hayle.

NTG – Page 59 – map. Hayle Youth Hostel is closed.

| 28 | Hayle to St Ives | OS 203 (T) Hayle (B.Rail) (V) Lelant (B.Rail) |

Grading: Moderate   Distance-   9   362   5   225

See also our Hayle to Zennor Path Description

Distance is measured from Hayle, around the estuary to Lelant then along the coast to St Ives.

Note between Lelant and Marazion there is a cross peninsula path, St Michael's Way. This could be used to make a circular round trip around Penwith by walking round the coast and then coming back inland from Penzance or Marazion to Carbis Bay.

In Hayle you can walk along the grass on the right hand side of the road. Just before the viaduct turn right to join the main road again on the other side of the creek. The quickest but dreariest route is straight along the main road, 'Carnsew Road'. There is a longer but somewhat more attractive alternative not to be missed by bird watchers. Go along the road passing the 30 decontrol sign and at the end of the long building on the right is a footpath sign-posted The Weir 1/2 a mile. At the end of tall hedge swing right, then swing left by a bridge. Then as the ground widens swing left again to walk along a lagoon embankment. Presently you come out again on the main road and have to turn right. Whichever way you did that first stretch from Hayle, turn right on the A3074 sign-posted St Ives passing the Old Quay House.

Here again is decision time as for some incredible reason the official path continues along the A3074 road through Lelant. At the end of the main street, where the main road swings left, you go ahead on a minor road to the church. If you wish to do this O.K. but we suggest a quieter and no further distance alternative below.

After the Old Quay House go carefully along the main road passing under the railway bridge. Then turn right signposted BR St Ives Park and Ride. You go along minor road, pass through a car park passing Lelant Saltings Station. You can then walk either along the road eastwards or for a while through the playing fields. If the tide is out you can go right to the end and use the poor stepping stones. If tide is in join the road earlier because the stones get covered by the tide. Then follow the road which turns inland coming out by the church.

At the church notice the unusual blocks which are used for walling at the west gate. They are old slag foundry blocks from Hayle. Continuing on the same line go ahead across the golf course and under the railway again. Here turn left to proceed along the seaward side of the railway.

Just before Carrack Gladden where you are close to the sea there are several paths going down on to the beach. If the tide is well out you can go down and save your self several ups and downs by walking along the beach to Carbis Bay.

If you stay on the path you come up by a pedestrian level crossing and then swing right, on the descent avoid two beach paths on your right.

About two hundred yards before Carbis Bay there is another opportunity to drop to go down to the beach and save yourself one last hill. If you stay with the path you go up to join a road, turn right down this. Circle round behind the cafe complex to leave Carbis Bay on a tarmac path above the beach but below the hotel.

Ascend, crossing a railway footbridge then keep ahead avoiding path on left. Continue along ignoring 'Private road pedestrians only' on right. The path becomes a minor road where road swings left and there is another private road on your right go ahead. Cross the railway again on a more substantial old fashioned bridge to swing right and downhill. You come down to Porthminster Cafe and then you can walk either side of the little park, continuing along below the railway station.

NTG – Photographs pages 56 and 57 incorrectly printed in reverse.

| 29 | St Ives to Pendeen Watch | OS 203 (T) St Ives (B.Rail) |

Grading: Severe Distance- 21 383 13 238

See also our Hayle to Zennor and Zennor to Sennen Cove Path Descriptions

You are now starting on the longest and most deserted stretch of coast on the whole South West Way. Therefore think about accommodation. Out of season you will have to walk three whole sections, 22 miles, even in season two sections, 17 miles before you find refreshment on the path. You can divert as listed below inland but this will increase the mileage and all suggestions are subject to some seasonal closing and opening hours. There is not even a telephone box on the path. It is magnificent walking but do not start out unprepared.

Refreshment possibilities are, Zennor, Pendeen/Botallack and St Just. Then sometimes on the path is a mobile snack wagon in Cape Cornwall car park.

One other warning, the terrain is severe and in places after rain surprisingly boggy, few will average 2 miles an hour, in other words it will take you longer than you expect.

Many use St Ives as a staging post, if however you should just wish to walk through continue along the path below the railway station by which you enter. This becomes a tarmac lane which proves to be called 'The Warren' at its end. Keep as close as you can to the harbour until you reach its north west corner. Here you have a choice; the purists will stay with the harbour and walk out round what is called The Island or St Ives Head, it is a pleasant walk. The less pure or perhaps those with still a lot of miles to cover can cut the corner by following signs to 'Tate Gallery' this will bring them out behind Porthmeor Beach.

Those going out to the Island can walk right round the harbour to turn left signposted 'The Museum'. Normally you can continue along a path past the Museum but that is likely to be closed until 1996 for major drainage works. You therefore have to take evasive action through narrow streets to come out to the grassy island.

You can walk round the Island but the interesting little St Nicholas Chapel is on the high point in the middle. When you have completed your circuit you turn right to pass along in front of the 'Tate Gallery'.

Go along behind the beach passing the 'Tate Gallery' ignoring the ramp going down to the beach. The road starts to rise, there is a car park on your right and the path you want starts to bear off right by some public conveniences. You pass a bowling green and continue along the deteriorating tarmac path out into the country.

One place where it is easy to go wrong, because of inadequate signposting, is shortly after Clodgy Point on Burthallan Cliff a path goes inland here and currently it is better marked than the main coastal path.

The coastal path cuts behind the NT property of Pen Enys Point if you should have time on your hands it is a pleasant extension.

If the weather is clear Carn Naun Point is the place to look back and gloat at what you have done. Be careful though a little later just before the stream, where there is a path down to beach which you should avoid, and, just after the stream a path running inland which ignore. Look for seals out on the Carracks they are often there.

You pass the old mine building at Treen Cove and come out behind Gurnard's Head. Here again if you have time it is a splendid diversion out to the Head but so often folk are pressed for time and cut across the neck.

The area around Porthmeor Cove is particularly spectacular if you can take your eyes briefly off where you are putting your feet!

Bosigran is difficult to negotiate and we have asked the N.T. for better signing. As you drop off Carn Veslan look ahead to the ridge of Bosigran Cliff and aim for the inland high point. (Not the big hill inland with the tower.) The path drops then starts to swing left uphill, crosses through a ruined wall then forks right (not the obvious path going up left). Shortly you do go left up another clear path but in only a few yards turn right up a more indistinct path heading for the inland high point. As you get nearer you pass round to the left of it to drop into the valley. Here you go across a main track used by the climbers and on across a little stone bridge. You go straight up the other side only swinging right again as you approach the top wall.

On Rosemergy cliff there is a currently unmarked four cross way footpath junction, go straight ahead.

| 30 | Pendeen Watch to Cape Cornwall | OS 203 Inland (V) St Just |

| Grading: Moderate | Distance- | 6 | 389 | 4 | 242 |

See also our Zennor to Sennen Cove Path Description

Remember what was said about refreshment in section 29.

The official path from Pendeen Watch goes along the road to the end of the next block of buildings and here turns right. There is a better unofficial coastal route which you can find by walking along to the right of the road and going down along the cliffs as the road swings away from the coast. Naturally avoid the marked and fenced off mineshaft. Presently you come opposite a close inshore islet The Avarack with a big cairn on the top. Here take the mid path going downhill, not the one right on cliff top. Towards the bottom the path swings left again up a stream valley to rejoin the official route at a bridge over the stream.

After the Levant Mine the path swings right along tracks which are not coastal and what few signs there are you may trip over but are unlikely to see! However do watch for the turning out to Kenidjack Castle it has a long history of not being properly signed and many miss it.

Out on Kenidjack Castle the path goes down across a stile and reaches a track where you are signed left. The adventurous may prefer to turn right a couple of yards and go down across the old spoil heaps, later keeping close to the cliffs on the right to reach the stream. Cross the stream, circle round the right side of the spoil heaps on the other side and go up a faint path to an old leat, dried up stream bed. Turn briefly right along this to clamber up a few more yards to another leat unfortunately more overgrown of late but passable. Turn right along this to reach the road just before Cape Cornwall.

If you are not adventurous turn left as signed presently veering right downhill. Continue up the valley by a cottage to swing right and cross a footbridge. The path then swings right to a junction by a ditch. The official path swings left zig-zagging uphill to turn right at the top. An easy but somewhat overgrown in places alternative continues right. If you take this proceed along the path, just before a small piece of ruined wall on your left, scramble up a few yards to turn right on a similar path above which leads to the road.

When you reach the road whichever way you came you must turn down it. The official path goes down towards Cape Cornwall but does not go out on to it. Therefore those in a hurry may prefer to turn left just before the car park, but careful if you want refreshment, the snack wagon, if it is there, will be down in the car park. Alternatively if you have the time, go out on the Cape it is a wonderful spot owned by N.T. for 57 good reasons and open to all. It was once considered to be 'Lands End' so may be it has had a lucky escape!

31	**Cape Cornwall to Sennen Cove**				**OS 203**

Grading: Moderate	Distance-	8	397	5	247

See also our Zennor to Sennen Cove Path Description

After Cape Cornwall you climb up the track to Ballowal Barrow, the road swings off left but the Coast Path goes ahead.

In the Porth Nanven valley you cross the stream; do not turn seawards but head up opposite towards the little col. The path then goes straight ahead above the sea.

At Carr, Barges the path takes a little inland loop to avoid the worst of the sand dunes. If the tide is out a quicker option is to walk along the firm sand to Sennen Cove.

32	**Sennen Cove to Porthcurno**			**OS 203 (V) Sennen Cove**

Grading: Moderate	Distance-	10	407	6	253

See also our Sennen Cove to Porthcurno Path Description

Leaving Sennen Cove you pass the Round House; go on into the car park area and turn left at the public toilets. Proceed ahead shortly to turn right and then head for the battlemented look-out.

Paths from Sennen to Land's End and for several miles beyond are so ubiquitous that it is impossible usually to give precise directions, you just follow the coast and your fancy and are unlikely to go seriously astray. There has in time past been publicity in the national press about footpath access to Land's End. This in no way concerns the Coast Path which is as freely available as it has been for years past.

Regarding the Land's End complex itself, you have two choices, if you want to use the cafes or other facilities head straight for it. If you wish to pretend it is not there, though that may be difficult, keep right out on the coast and only look out to sea! For what it is worth the official route goes via Gleeb Cottage with its collection of animals rather than using the path nearer the sea.

The short length just before Nanjizal Cove is perhaps the best bit of a very fine section, if you are lucky enough to pass that way in early spring you will see that it was once a bulb growing area. After you have crossed the stream do not turn right at once but proceed ahead for 30 to 40 yards then turn right.

You can if, you are pushed, completely cut off Gwennap Head and Tol-Pedn-Penwith however try not to do so. Tol-Pedn means the holed headland and it is spectacular. To find the hole proceed up to the look-out house and just pass it to stand in front of the old rocket practice wooden pole. From here walk on a bearing of approx 140 and go for about 40 yards over the brow, the path then swings right 190, you drop down over a natural bridge with the hole on your left. Walk round it, do not fall down it! and then leave again on obvious path which soon climbs back on the clifftop, you do not have to go back the way you came.

At Porthgwarra, if you turn down the slipway it is possible to make a short diversion by way of a tunnel through which boats were once hauled. The only snag with this innocent entertainment is that you will have by-passed the seasonal cafe above! If you use the cafe turn first right afterwards.

Although the path from Porthgwarra leaves by an inland route you can walk out round Carn Scathe if you wish. To do this when you have turned down from the cafe swing right just before granite gate posts between the cliff top and a garden. The first few yards are overgrown but you will soon be glad you went that way. When you get back to main path turn right of course.

You come out into the car park behind the Minack Theatre through an unusual kissing gate. Go through the car park to leave at the other end on a path parallel and behind the Theatre entrance. There are various warning notices but you would need to be very infirm not to be able to go down the steps. At the bottom turn left and do not, unless you want a swim, go down to the beach but keep along the path contouring above the beach.

In Porthcurno there is a good cafe usually open from Easter to the end of the season but you will have to make a short detour left up the valley to reach it.

---

33   Porthcurno to Lamorna   OS 203

Grading: Strenuous   Distance-   8   415   5   258

See also our Porthcurno to Penzance Path Description

There is again fine walking in this section and some of it easy going, however parts of it are not easy and it may well take longer than you expect.

If you have visited the cafe you can take the old path and miss out Percella Point but the views from it over Porthcurno are spectacular. After Percella Point the official path keeps inland for a while but the NT have a path which loops out around the next headland returning to the Coast Path further West.

The next chance of a diversion is Treryn Dinas which is an extra not to be missed by anyone who likes a scramble, up and on to the famous Logan Rock.

Unfortunately you have to go back inland again to continue on your way to Penberth, a scenic gem. Cross the slipway, passing the old capstan and go up the other side outside the house to turn left at the top.

Around St Loy the authorities have so far failed to make the good path they should, you therefore get shunted inland then have to use what in wet weather can be a very mucky path to get to the beach. There is no path at all for a few yards you have to boulder hop along the shore but do watch out for the turn inland again after about 50 metres. We have had reports of a walker missing this in misty weather and getting cut off by the tide.

After Boscawen Point and before Tater-du Lighthouse you come to a junction; do not turn left but proceed ahead to go through two large metal green gates, neither of which were signed on last check.

Be careful on Carn Barges not to be diverted onto the inland path to Lamorna, the better route is round the coast. Look for the cross just before Lamorna unless you are in too much of a rush to get to the seasonal cafe, right on the path!

| Grading: Strenuous and then easy | Distance- | 10 | 425 | 6 | 264 |

See also our Porthcurno to Penzance Path Description

After the cafe you swing right behind the harbour and cross the bridge. You go up past a most complicated waymark which, unless you look at it carefully, almost sends you the wrong way. However keep right but with only one house still on your right.

The path is then good out around Carn-du and on to Kemyel Point. The route from there to Mousehole is not good because the authorities have ignored the old coastal path with its still extant stone stiles in favour of a sinuous new route and then a rural lane.

You climb the hill to pass a onetime look-out on your right. The path steadily improves underfoot and eventually you come out on to a road where turn right.

Few find the right route into Mousehole because it is never signed properly. We will describe it here in case you would like to join that exclusive bunch. Descend the hill passing the Wild Bird Hospital on your left. There is a post box on your right with a Coast Path sign pointing the way you have come but not the way you are going! Turn right at an acute angle opposite Kemyel Cottage. Go down a narrow tarmac lane 140 degrees part way down bear slightly left heading towards the rocks, St Clement's Isle, you can see out to sea. Just before the foreshore swing left along a terrace and fork right into a car park. Go to the bottom right end of the car park to continue briefly along the harbour side. You then have to turn in again left and then first right. However those with an interest in history before turning right should go forward past the house with pillars to read the plaque on the other side. The turn right brings you out on to a busier street bear right along it to come behind the harbour again.

The official route leaving Mousehole goes up a narrow road without pavements but we suggest you do not. At the other end of the harbour go in and pass through the car park there, down a ramp and along a concrete path. Go round the corner and up steps past a lifebuoy at the top turn right along the pavement.

Approaching Newlyn, as you are a pedestrian you can use the No Entry or, even better, if you watch closely there is a footpath on the right going down a slope just before it and you can go safely the same way at low level.

Go round the back of Newlyn Harbour passing the War memorial then swing right over the little bridge, Seaman's Mission on the right. Over the bridge bear right to come out once again behind the beach. After you have passed the tennis courts or remains of them the path comes back to the road, here go across the corner of the beach to go up steps and walk along the promenade. At the end of the Promenade pass the swimming pool and continue round to pass Penzance Harbour and on to the railway station.

BMG – Does not cover complete path or mileage through Penzance.

| Grading: Easy | Distance- | 5 | 430 | 3 | 267 |

See also our Penzance to Porthleven Path Description

Note between Lelant and Marazion there is a cross peninsula path St Michael's Way. This could be used to make a circular round trip around Penwith by walking round the coast and then coming back inland from Penzance or Marazion to Carbis Bay.

You leave Penzance from the bottom of Market Jew St. going out on the main road alongside the railway station, however the pavement runs out on the seaward side so it is better for a while to keep to the landward. When you get to B3311 cross over later joining the A30 at the end of the Penzance ring road. Soon on your right just before the heliport is a footbridge, cross this and the coast path goes along the top of the sea wall, if the tide is out you can walk along the beach as an alternative.

At Long Rock where the station is now a restaurant you debouch into the car park. Go through this and continue along the road towards Marazion. There is a roadside car park and then the path goes up on the sand dunes, although at last check there was no sign and no apparent way up. Press on between the beach and the road, if you get this bit right you will cross a pedestrian bridge just seaward of the road bridge. You now go through field/car parks going up at the end a side road to join the main road.

36 Marazion to Prussia Cove OS 203 (V) Marazion

Grading: Moderate   Distance-   6   436   4   271

See also our Penzance to Porthleven Path Description

Walkers are treated badly at the beginning of this section, there is no path at all for a while and then the first coastal length is on a beach.

You go up the road in Marazion, zig-zagging if you wish to use a pavement and pass the 40 sign. When just ahead is the sign which thanks you for driving carefully turn right into a driveway. At the bottom you are on a beach, walk along to ascend some hideous metal steps.

Shortly above Trenow Beach if you are fortunate you will be able to walk along a cliff top path without trouble.

After that you should have no trouble getting to Perranuthnoe where there are refreshments in season. The path turns inland here behind some houses, comes out on to the road to go up the lane opposite. Go right at the fork passing Blue Burrow Cottage and swing right.

When you get back to the coast do not go down the track to the beach but turn left into the next field. At Cudden Point the path cuts slightly inland but then the true coast path goes seaward again before Little Cudden.

At Bessie's Cove the path goes up to join a track by a letter box. Continue ahead bearing right to turn right over a stone stile beside a massive gate. You can go down the track but the path is correct and at the top is traffic free.

37 Prussia Cove to Porthleven OS 203

Grading: Moderate   Distance-   10   446   6   277

See also our Penzance to Porthleven Path Description

The path at Prussia Cove is quite a surprise, a sunken lane between two large stone buildings. You continue along a lane with the old coastguard row up on your left to pass through a gate, after which the track becomes a path and you should fork right at the first junction.

The path later becomes a green track down to Praa Sands where there are plenty of opportunities for refreshment in season.

The presently poorly marked route takes you down on the beach to leave it again as soon as you have passed the beach cafes up wooden steps. At the top turn right and proceed along to turn left to the well marked path through the sand dunes, shortly to turn right along the road through the estate.

If you do not wish to go down on the beach there is nothing to stop you turning left after the first cafe you come to, go inland past the public conveniences and then turning back right through the car park to reach the coast. Then proceed as above from the top of the wooden steps. If you like beach walking and the tide is out you can walk the length of the beach.

Assuming you have gone through the estate swing right at the other end to pick up the path just inland of the big stones in the road.

At Rinsey Head the path swings inland cutting off the point. You pass an old railway coach and at the top turn left and then immediately right going through the N.T. car park. As you drop down you should see two paths ahead, one going uphill which you do not want, the other going down, which you do. Pass the restored engine house to pick up the path below it on the other side.

At Trewavas Head the path swings inland of the old mine ruins, this used to be difficult to follow but recently way-marking has been improved.

As you approach Porthleven the path becomes semi-tarmac. You pass a cross erected in memory of those buried on the cliffs in unconsecrated ground. You go through a gate, or round the gatepost to join a lane, swing right as you reach the main road to go down to the harbour.

---

38   Porthleven to Mullion Cove   OS 203 (V) Porthleven

Grading: Moderate		Distance-	12	458	7	284

See also our Porthleven to The Lizard Path Description

At Porthleven as so often you have to walk right round the back of the harbour and out the other side. You go beyond the battlemented tower like building to keep up the coastal road using Mounts Road although it says it is a cul-de-sac.

Shortly after the last building on the right turn left off the track into the N.T. property Parc-an-als Cliff to avoid a landfall. Over the top you pick up the track again to proceed on and down to the beach.

If you have plenty of time there is a walking route right around Loe Pool the biggest natural lake in Cornwall.

As you cross Loe Bar look for the path going up just to the right of the field but divert to see the white cross on your right. You pick up the path you want on 126 degrees from the cross, after the path levels out you pass a wooden seat and about 180 yards after this fork right to pick up the old route.

At Gunwalloe Fishing Cove you come out on to gravelly road, do not take the first right which goes down to the beach but swing right on the second turning to pass inland of a house. At the top of the hill there is a stile where walking gardeners should look left.

Above Halzephron Cove you swing round to join the old road. Turn right shortly before you come to a barrier. You enter N.T. Halzephron Cliff do not turn right immediately but continue ahead to turn right just before the next field gate.

At Gunwalloe Church Cove there is an option. If you want to see the church, and it is interesting, when you join the road go right and after you have seen church you can usually cross the beach and its stream.

If a church visit is not for you the correct route swings left aiming for buildings which prove to be public conveniences and a very seasonal cafe. There is a sign where you join the road but it is badly sited so is not obvious. Proceed down the road with N.T. Gunwalloe Towans sign on your right. Bear left off the road just before a turning space. Cross a bridge over a stream and turn right round the back of the beach. The path is narrow until you come to a track where turn left uphill.

At the top there is a small car park; as soon as you have gone through this you can swing right to walk along the cliff tops and so miss a length of tarmac road.

There is a seasonal cafe at Poldhu Cove. You walk round the back of the beach on the road and go up the drive of the residential care home. Turn right off the driveway shortly before you get to the big house.

Skirt around the back of Polurrian Cove to go up the steps, then a track to turn right on a road. Where the road swings left proceed ahead on a path. If you are a purist the coast path goes in front of old coastguard look out, but this bit of path is seldom cleared.

Just past the Mullion Cove Hotel the path veers right, through the car parking spaces opposite starting by an old cannon. At the bottom turn left.

---

39   Mullion Cove to Lizard   OS 203

Grading: Moderate		Distance-	10	468	6	290

See also our Porthleven to The Lizard Path Description

Very spectacular a wonderful section this, with lots of interest. It can be accomplished too, without great effort! Unless the weather is beastly you will certainly enjoy this stretch. If you can arrange the transport it makes a spectacular long half day excursion.

You go up the road a very little way turn right and then right again.

After Mullion Cove several places there have alternative paths but usually it makes little difference which you take, except as mentioned below.

After Parc Bean Cove going up Lower Predannock Cliff you want the higher path not the lower and at the top bear right.

After Vellan Cliff just before Gew-Graze the path veers slightly inland for a stile.

The path down to Kynance has not been well signed for some years. If that is still the case, as you go down aim for the further headland you can see which is Lizard Point. Later you will see a sign close to the sea where you have to turn left, go down further to cross a wide concrete bridge by a house.

There is a good, long season cafe at Kynance Cove. Unless the tide is right in, the quickest route is to cross the few yards at the back of the beach and go up the steps the other side. If the tide is right in you have to go up the drive before the cafe and swing right at the top.

Whichever way you came go through the car park and go out again just to the right of the public toilets.

Lizard Town is exceptionally well foot-pathed so if you are lodging there you have a great many options.

40 | Lizard to Coverack — OS 203 and 204 1 mile to (V) Lizard Town

Grading: Moderate but strenuous in parts   Distance-   18   486   11   301

See also our The Lizard to Helford Path Description

A word of warning; old stone stiles are made of the local serpentine which can prove very slippery when wet, so take care on wet polished rock.

Most folk will start this walk by turning left above the Most Southerly Cafe, going along in front of the lighthouse. Unless you suffer from vertigo do not miss diverting right shortly after the lighthouse to see the spectacular Lion's Den which although only about 20 yards off the path is still missed by many.

You pass Housel Bay Hotel and later go through a kissing gate just before a longish asbestos type building. Look for the small plaque just beyond it. The path is odd in that it keeps to the top edge of field until the next gate, where it swings to the seaward edge again.

You pass the old Lloyd's Signal Station and come out on a drive by a house. You go along this drive only a short way and the coast path then takes off right.

At Kilcobben Cove you come just inland of the top building of the life-boat station, walk round it and go down the first little flight of steps but then go forward and not down the long flight of steps to the life-boat!

At Church Cove you go across diagonally behind one building to go through a big gate. You should avoid the first turning right and the next turn into the quarry.

After Polgwidden watch for a sharp right turn going along in front of an isolated house. The wrong path goes forward and looks more impressive and, despite numerous requests, there has not been a sign here in years.

Those with a taste for adventure and a resilience to scratches may like to divert down the cliff on the southern end of The Devil's Frying Pan before Cadgwith. It is possible to go over the top of the natural arch and so down to the bottom of the pit. This is the way really to appreciate the size of this natural feature but we stress it is only for the adventurous.

You pass the N.T. Devil's Frying Pan sign and the true coast path is diagonally ahead, down steps into the car park and out the other end to turn right. In fact it has lately been signposted avoiding the car park; the choice is yours. Whichever way you go you drop down a lovely path through a garden. Watch for the right turn just after you have gone over a stone stile next to a metal gate.

You drop into Cadgwith behind the beach, chance of refreshment, and then start up the hill swinging left with the road to turn first right just past Veneth Cottage.

After Enys Head there is a poorly marked section, you come to a fork where go left, soon there is another right turn which you ignore, you come down to a gate where then turn right. Go down for some while till you see N.T. Poltesco sign on left. Here turn right going down steps and over a bridge. Avoid both the next right turns unless you wish to see the old Poltesco serpentine works.

At next junction as you go up bear right. Later you go through a golf course area at the end of which swing right. You come out on a road where turn right. If the road is busy you can presently go across and take a permissive path to the beach, but it is not as rewarding as you might hope.

At Kennack Sands, refreshments in season, the path swings behind the beach up towards the toilets and then is now well marked behind the two beaches. If the tide is well out you can walk along both beaches to the far end but as the proper path at time of writing is well maintained there is little gained unless you want a swim!

What you do need to watch for at the far end of second beach is that you take the coast path which looks fairly insignificant starting up nearly on cliff edge, there is a bigger wide path going inland but do not take it. There is another junction shortly where keep right again.

Care should be taken in front of Borgwitha and behind the cliff castle Carrick Luz because you cut across the neck of the peninsula and do not go inland or seaward. Improved waymarking should mean that you do not now go astray.

There is a very steep if scenic drop to Dowlais Cove and up the other side. After Beagles Point there is another smaller drop, cross a bridge and go up what is almost a stone chute the other side. At the top turn right.

After Black Head there is a very fine viewpoint for looking ahead along the South Cornish Coast. The path has been much improved and for a long way goes along the top of the cliffs. After you pass a piggery the route gets complicated. You come to a track, bear left but after about thirty yards go ahead on a path where the track swings left.

You cross an old stone stile, pass an old fashioned pump and come to a grassy area with caravans*. Here swing sharp right and turn right again when you get to the macadam drive. Go along the left side of this until just before a sign forbidding access. Here turn sharp left and go down steps; there is a junction here left which is a quick but incorrect route. Right is correct and more scenic. Go down to next junction where ahead is Chynall's Point, a cul-de sac but part of the Coast Path. Left is your route towards Coverack.

As you enter Coverack you reach a tarmac path, turn right and go down to join a road. If you wish to do all the Coast Path there is then a little loop that many miss. Twenty yards down the road the path goes away right above a children's playground. The path then looks as though it is going to end but press on over a slight rise to go down steps and turn left in front of a house. Keep right of the back of a pub into the car park turn left and left again to pass the front of the same pub.

*There is a shorter alternative route here if the hour is late or the blisters painful. Swing right as above but when you get to the drive turn left along it and very soon divert off right on a field path to Coverack.

41	**Coverack to Helford**			**OS 204 (V) Coverack**		

Grading: Moderate   Distance-   20   506   13   314

See also our The Lizard to Helford Path Description

The statistically minded may wish to be advised that in this section they will pass the halfway mark of the whole coast path. For those just walking sections at random this may not matter much., To those hardier, or perhaps we should say, foolhardy souls who are trying to walk the whole path, this is indeed a point of significance. The only thing we need add is that it does not matter which way you are going there is an enormous amount of very good walking ahead.

In Coverack you walk around behind the harbour and the beach and where the main road swings inland go ahead up the small tarmac road. The tarmac ends just before a small rise, go over this and start to drop down looking for a path turning off right just before a gate across the road.

The path out to Lowland Point is improved but the further you go the less evidence of path there is. However the basic ploy is to go along, keeping close to the shore going east until you have to turn north at the point.

After Lowland Point the Coast Path goes through Dean Quarry. Your Association fought hard to get the path on the coast here rather than a long diversion inland.

Most of the quarry area is well signposted, but it is important that when you come up level with the first building you start down the steep ramp to the beach the footpath goes left off this. Towards the end of the quarry area signs are more scarce but keep with the track close above the sea to go down on to the beach at Godrevy Cove.

Walk just over half way along the beach crossing the stream bed which sometimes has water but is often dry, then turn half left to circumvent a marshy area and pick up the path at the back of the beach. Here turn left until you can turn inland through fields. At present the correct path is a sunken, usually muddy, lane on your right, so that most folk stay in the fields to join the track up to Rosenithon.

At the T junction in Rosenithon turn right, go up the hill the road swings right and just after this the footpath takes off left into a field. Cross one field and a traditional Cornish stile, surely the forerunner of the modern cattle grid. Cross two more fields in the same direction and surprisingly the stile is just below the gate you come to!

Turn left on the road then first right down into Porthoustock. From Porthoustock to Porthallow the official route again goes inland to avoid the now unused quarries around Pencra Head and Porthkerris Point. However we understand that locals and those who have no knowledge of exactly what a definitive path is walk through this second lot of quarries although of course they should not!

You leave Porthoustock up the hill, but soon, where the road swings right go ahead on a track. You pass houses on your right, the track ends and you keep ahead into a field. Here turn steeply up the field 302 degrees joining the right hand field bank at the top. Proceed ahead to a sunken stile in the corner then slightly more right 338 degrees to another sunken stile just left of the gate.

Bear left on the road which later bears left to Trenance where turn right. At the next T junction look for the footpath ahead and a few yards to your right. Go down alongside a vineyard to join the road where turn right down to Porthallow. There are seasonal refreshments available here.

You leave Porthallow by taking the second turning on to the beach and immediately turning left to go along the back of the foreshore and up steps, bearing right at the first junction.

As you approach Nare Point ignore a metal kissing gate which you pass on the right to shortly turn left along a one time track which served the lookout. You go through a gate and when the track swings uphill proceed ahead.

You pass N.T. The Herra property, come to a small beach where go across the back. You come to a second beach where you turn right on a path behind the beach.

A very short distance beyond the beach a footpath takes off left and it is decision time. If you know the tide is in and you want to walk round turn left!

Walking Round.
It is about 2¼ miles easy walking but nearly all road. This distance is extra to the mileage shown for the section. If time is of the essence you can go via Manaccan and be in Helford in 3 miles but that is of course not walking the Coast Path!

The actual route soon becomes tarmac then takes off right to go through one field. In the second field the path does not go up to the farm buildings but skews right across the field to run along the far side of field hedge and then comes back to the farm track to go up to the road. At the road turn right and then right again at Carne at the head of the creek.

Gillan Creek Crossing
No ferry but it can usually be forded from one hour before Low Tide to one hour after. Predicted low water is 15 minutes earlier than shown in the Tide Tables. But do proceed with care!

There are two possible crossing places. Proceed until you can go no further along the path by the river, descend steps to the beach and wade across towards two caravans on far shore.

A little further upstream you can cross part way on stepping stones. But this is not the easy option it sounds because they are extremely slippery and do not go across the whole river. Our Association has asked for improvement here.

Once across, turn right to pass in front of church, there is an attractive collection box you might care to notice and even use just in front.

Turn left up the hill and about ten yards past a mounting block on the left look for a path going off at an angle right, take this and turn first right. You may then see the sign which should be at the bottom.

If you have plenty of time the circular route out around Dennis Head is rewarding. However there is a legitimate alternative across the neck of the peninsula. In either case you then have a short section in fields before the long wooded stretch along the Helford River.

You come out by an old railed hound enclosure to swing slightly right and then go up a tar-mac drive with grass in the centre. At the top turn right down the road, turn left up steps just as you get to the drive of a house called Traeth Cottage. It is easy to miss, if you get to the shore you have missed it!

Go along the back of the car park, down the road, crossing the first bridge over the creek. Turn right and go along past The Shipwright's Arms to the ferry point.

42	**Helford to Falmouth**			**OS 204 (V) Helford**	

Grading: Moderate	Distance-	15	521	10	324

See also our Helford to Place Path Description

Helford to Helford Passage use ferry, see details below. If the ferry is not running your alternatives are probably a taxi or 8¹/₂ mile walk. This is mostly road but you can incorporate Frenchman's Creek.

Helford Passage (Helford River). Seasonal.
Cove Boats, Helford Passage,
Nr Falmouth Tel Mawnan Smith
01326 250116

Good Friday to 31 Oct incl. Departs Helford Passage on the hour and Helford at 10 min. past the hour, more often as demand increases. All ferry crossings are subject to tide and weather conditions.

This section makes a good day walk from Falmouth by using the, admittedly infrequent, bus service to the road turn just above Helford Passage. Be sure you get your bus out and walk back, that way you can enjoy your walk.

At Helford Passage go along the beach eastwards to go up the steps at the end. At Durgan swing sharp right when you reach the track then swing left by the old school. Go up the road past a little picnic area then DO NOT turn first right, it is the second turning you want.

At the next beach you come to Porth Saxon, you go in front of the boathouse, and the path is then at the back of the shore. At the following beach Porthallack the path in contrast stays in the fields to go on to the beach beyond a building.

The true Coast Path goes out round Rosemullion Head with its fine views but there is a short cut across its neck. You come to the N.T. Nansidwell property and although it does not look like it the path exit is in the bottom right hand corner of the field. There is another path better walked going ahead but it is the wrong path. The path does not go on beach but swings left at the last moment.

You come out on to the road at Maenporth (refreshments in season) turn right along the road turning right again at the other end of the beach.

On reaching the road turn right for Swanpool, there walk across the back of the beach to continue on the Coast Path turning right at first junction. At Gyllyngvase Beach turn right along the road it will not be most people's favourite walking but it is quite rewarding looking back to where you have previously been.

When you get towards the end of the seafront passing the last big hotel, The Falmouth Hotel, do not then go down right but continue on the pavement beside the road until you have passed the cul-de-sac notice, then you can swing right if you wish away from the road. However presently you will need to cross the road for the safety of the pavement around Pendennis Point.

At the point the road swings left, go along this road for about quarter of a mile, passing three seats, then just before the fourth seat there are steps going down. There are three entries opposite, you want the third one, you come out on a tarmac lane briefly left then turn right on the road. You go down with interesting views over the shipyards.

You come to a T junction where turn right, go ahead at the junction under the railway bridge. It does sign town centre left but that is the long way for traffic so stay with us! The road shortly swings right and there is a pub on the left which still proclaims it has hotel stables and motor garage! The road swings right and there is plenty of interest.

You pass a big car park on your right and it soon becomes a shopping street. Continue right up it passing Marks & Spencers, there are not many of them on the Coast Path! and the next turning on the right takes you to the ferry.

BMG – Does not cover the total mileage through Falmouth.

| 43 | Falmouth to Place House | OS 204 (T) Falmouth (B.Rail) (V) St Mawes |

No Grading

Distance-   0   521   0   324

See also our Falmouth to Portloe Path Description

In season you can cross by using two ferries, see details below. The only point to watch is that depending on conditions the first ferry takes 20 to 30 minutes for the passage.

The ferry from Falmouth to St Mawes runs the whole year round except for winter Sundays. The scarcity of public transport in winter on Sundays combined with the fact that it is a long hike makes us advise anyone arriving in Falmouth on a Sunday to take it as a day off!

The ferry from St Mawes to Place only runs in season. If you are a purist there is a reasonable walking route round of 8–9 miles two sections of which are very good walking indeed, see below for details. There are about a couple of buses a day from St Mawes to Gerrans, except on Sundays, or you could consider a taxi. If the ferry is not in service you can always ask. We have heard from walkers who have been lucky enough to get a lift from local boat owners.

Falmouth/St Mawes
St Mawes Ferry Co.,
75 The Beacon, Falmouth, TR11 2BD
Tel: (01326) 313813 – Nov–March
(01326) 313201 – April–Oct
(01850) 769127 (mobile)

All year round. Weather permitting.
Falmouth/St Mawes (Summer Service)
Weekdays: 0830 hrs, 0945 hrs, then 1/2 hourly
to 1715 hrs. Sundays (commencing May)
1000 to 1700 hrs. Hourly. Depart Falmouth,
Prince of Wales Pier. St Mawes/Falmouth.
Weekdays 0900, 0945, then 1/2 hourly until
1715 hrs. Sundays (commencing May)
1030 to 1730 hrs. Hourly
Nov. to March boats daily. From Falmouth
0830, 1015, 1115, 1315, 1415, 1615 hrs.
From St Mawes 0900, 1045, 1145, 1345,
1445, 1645 hrs. No Sunday Service.

The St Mawes Ferry Co. are prepared to land pre-organized parties of 20 or more at Place House. To do this they would need prior knowledge to lay on an extra boat. This is also dependent on the state of the tide and weather.

St Mawes/Place House (St Anthony)
For information please write to:
Mr R Balcombe
75 Drump Road
Redruth TR15 1PR
Tel: (01209) 214901

Seasonal
Daily – 1 May–30 September
St Mawes to Place 1/2 hourly
from 1000 to 1630 hrs. No 1300 boat. Place
to St Mawes 1/2 hourly from 1015 to 1645.
No 1315 boat.

Walking Route
Turn left after leaving the ferry from Falmouth and proceed along the road till you reach the castle, immediately after the castle take a left turn along a minor tarmac road, if you look carefully you will see a footpath sign amongst all the clutter about the Castle's car parks.

Follow this minor road until you come to the N.T. land 'Newton Cliff' which you enter. The route follows a very lovely path along the estuary with superb views across to Falmouth and the far shore. You come out on a minor tarmac road just after a footpath sign 'Public Footpath St Mawes 2 miles' pointing back the way one has come. Turn right along the road. Continue along this minor road bearing left at the junction to pass in front of a boatyard. Immediately after passing the boatyard buildings the path swings a few yards right to proceed along the bank above the shore.

You come to the gate leading to the churchyard with a large sign 'Dogs on Leads Please Consecrated Ground'. Go through this, keeping left all the way to pass the church on your right. Ignore the turning right marked 'Way out' but instead keep left through a lych gate and pass the house 'Lanzeague'. After its second gate the path bears right up hill starting beside a low rail fence backed by trees. You pass through a decrepit metal gate continuing ahead uphill with views of the creek to your left. You go through a wooden gate into a lane in parts muddy in parts green to exit on to the road.

Turn left and walk along the road for about 150 yds, ignore the first footpath on the right immediately past a house but take the second on the right shortly afterwards. For the first field you have the hedge on the right. For the second and third it is on your left. Then for the fourth it is again on your right. In this fourth field look for sharp right turn shortly before the end. Turn down steps to the road. Here turn right to reach the main A3078.

At Trethem Mill turn left, this is on a bridge crossing the creek, and immediately turn right up some stone steps and ascend through a wood. Coming out of the wood cross field on approximate bearing of 110, to leave by a conspicuous tree. Cross the corner of the next field on 140 and leave by a wooded track. At the top there is a stile bear 137 diagonally across field to hedge and follow this to road. Turn right down the road.

At the next junction follow the road curving round to the right past Polhendra Cottage and then left through a large metal gate as indicated by a footpath sign. Aim across approx. 123 to descend to the bottom of the hedge which you can see on the opposite side of the valley. Here you will find a bridge, cross it and proceed up, with the hedge on your left. At the top ascend some stone steps and cross the next two fields on 125. On reaching the road turn right into Gerrans.

Walk down to the church and here take the left fork (not left turn) Treloan Lane. You walk via Treloan and Rosteague, at each junction keeping straight ahead to come out on the road just before Porth Farm. The slightly quicker way is then to turn right along the road and left where there is a sign 'Footpath to Place by Percuil River' to come to a wooden bridge. The pleasanter alternative is to go ahead into the N.T. car park and then turn right to get to the same wooden bridge by paths.

Over the bridge the path turns right to follow Porth Creek and then the Percuil River, down to the low tide landing point for the ferry and soon on to Place itself. This last stretch of walking is very scenic.

NTG – There is a St Mawes to Place Ferry

| 44 | **Place House to Portscatho** | | | **OS 204** |

Grading: Easy   Distance-   10   531   6   330

See also our Falmouth to Portloe Path Description

The St Anthony Peninsula, thanks to the N.T., offers a very good half-day circular walk. Most people will start at Porth Farm walk to Place as already described and then follow the Coast Path round St Anthony's Head and on to Towan Beach here turning back inland to Porth Farm.

Some maps show a definitive right of way across the front of Place House, this route however is not really practical except at very low tides.

This means that you must walk up the road at Place passing the gates of the house and shortly turn right to go behind the church. You get back to the creekside, soon to leave it again to go over behind Amsterdam Point. The path then is superb with wonderful views across the Carrack Roads. After the footbridge across the top of a one time dam turn sharp right. Shortly turn even sharper left to go up steps and turn right again at the top. Look for the little path forking right up to the topograph for the best viewpoint.

The path then proceeds forwards without problems to Portscatho, however owing to the lie of the land you do not see the village until the very last moment and it always seems to take longer than one thinks it should!

Grading: Strenuous   Distance-   12   543   7   337

See also our Falmouth to Portloe Path Description

You leave Portscatho going through a couple of small fields if the tide is out you have a choice. You can start down the steps then turn right and go down to cross Porthcurnick Beach, this is slightly shorter. The reward for not turning for the beach but going up the steps opposite is that you then pass a seasonal refreshment hut.

Beyond Creek Stephen Point you have to descend right to the beach to turn along it for a very few yards before climbing once more. Eventually you cross a stile to get back to fields again.

A cliff fall, years ago, near the Nare Hotel and Cornwall County Council's failure to reinstate the path has led to a sign-posted diversion around the back. This involves a long and tedious walk by road through Gwendra. If the tide is out it is easier to walk along Pendower Beach to Carne Beach. You can look forward to see if this is feasible as you walk down by the car park before Pendower Beach.

Up to Carne Beach you may wonder why this stretch has been graded strenuous, you will soon cease to wonder!

Having ascended Nare Head it is possible to short cut it but unless the weather is poor do not do this or you will miss out on the rewarding views. Study the way the first arrow is pointing and follow its direction along the edge of the gorse. You pass another post and then come to a third which points left. Here, to get the best views of all, turn right to the head itself. You have though to come back the same way.

Return to the post on a bearing of 120 if you look carefully you will see a small path going forward into the gorse take this. This is the path which gives the best views of Gull Rock offshore. It winds back to join the track you would have joined anyway, here turn right.

At the other end of the track about 200 yds, where it opens up and there are what look like odd little ventilators, bear across right to pick up the coast again. If you go forward on the track you will arrive in the car park and miss the coast path.

Another place you can go wrong is after the very steep descent off The Blouth where the path swings left and then right over a stile. There is a sign but it is badly sited so it is easy to miss and as a result a lot of people go wrong here.

At The Straythe there is a pleasant surprise for those who walked this way some years ago. A new well engineered path zig-zags up to replace the old uncomfortable and nearly vertical flight of steps. At the top the route is well sign-posted through the gardens but you do need to turn right in the field when you get there.

There is a long descent into Portloe but at least you can see it unlike Portscatho. However watch for the sharp left turn just as you draw nearly level with a green seat on your right. Then you want the second turning on the left to pass in front of the public toilets and so down to Portloe.

| 46 | **Portloe to East Portholland** | **OS 204** |

Grading: Strenuous   Distance-   3   546   2   339

See also our Portloe to Mevagissey Path Description

This stretch is rewarding and will give you enjoyment for your efforts.

As you come up from the quay at Portloe you can turn first right, scramble along and up some steps, to rejoin the coast path that way. However the true coast path goes up the road, turns right along another road, and then shortly leaves it down some wide steps past cottages. The official route does have the advantage that it passes the Post Office which serves cream teas.

Recently there has been a coast path diversion signposted just before Perbargus Point. This has been occasioned by a minor landfall near but not on a low section of the path a few yards from West Portholland. When last walked there was no break in the path at all.

You can, if you wish, avoid the road walk from West to East Portholland by going forward behind the beach at West Portholland and walking along the sea wall between the two settlements. This is a little rocky at the beginning but should present no problems to any sure footed walker.

---

47 | East Portholland to Gorran Haven   OS 204

Grading: Moderate   Distance-   **11**   **557**   **6**   **345**

See also our Portloe to Mevagissey Path Description

The path starts along a one time tarmac lane from East Portholland. It turns right at the end of this lane to descend a field and continue alongside the coast. There is a path forward but if you use it, you simply get a longer stretch of road to walk to get to Porthluney Cove.

There is a seasonal cafe behind the beach in front of Caerhays Castle. Whether you have visited the cafe or not, note one point, on leaving the road you cross half across the first field joining a rough track close to a projecting corner of waste land. This track proceeds half right but the path itself turns sharp right along the fence. There is a marker post but it is badly sited in long grass and is often invisible.

From Hemmick Beach via The Dodman to Gorran Haven, it is all good walking; there are wonderful views from The Dodman in the right conditions. You can look back on triumphs past and challenges still long to come!

At Little Sand Cove there is an old path cutting the corner off Pen-a-Maen Point. We do not recommend it – you climb higher and will not have such good views.

---

48 | Gorran Haven to Mevagissey   OS 204 (V) Gorran Haven

Grading: Easy   Distance-   **5**   **562**   **4**   **349**

See also our Portloe to Mevagissey Path Description

This section starts happily enough but you are beginning to leave the most remote and least spoiled section of the South Cornish coast behind.

You come into Gorran Haven on Foxhole Lane, turn right into Canton and just before the beach turn left into Church St. Proceed up this, there is a footpath loop to the right if you want a brief better look at the beach, and turn right at the top into Cliff Road. You go up past the old coastguard row and turn right again at the top, still Cliff Road. At its end Cliff Road swings left and you go up a stile into a field.

From Turbot Point you descend to Colona Beach passing the N.T. Bodrugan's Leap sign. Swing right to pass behind the beach, do not swing left when the track swings left but proceed ahead very shortly to cross the tarmac drive to continue ahead on a footpath across the grass. At its start you are heading in a straight line for Mevagissey Harbour, later it veers a little left and you pick up a hedge on your right. Continue along this hedge until it goes up to join the road where you turn right.

At the end you will find the road is called Chapel Point Lane, turn right, swing left at the sea and follow the road round past the Rising Sun.

You swing right on entering Mevagissey on Polkirt Hill. You pass buildings on your right and then enter a park, proceed through this to the other end. Turn right down the first flight of public stone steps on the right to come out on the quay close to some public toilets.

Grading: Strenuous   Distance-   11   573   7   356

See also our Mevagissey to Fowey Path Description

In Mevagissey walk along the back of the harbour to turn right and then very shortly bear up left veering away from, and up above, the quayside.

You come out into open playing fields, go across but aim for the extreme right end of the buildings you see opposite. This is where the footpath leaves the field. There have been a series of landslips in the next section but no serious problems currently exist. Continue along, avoiding right turn down steps.

The path comes out again into a field and there is a steep descent to cross a bridge. Here turn left; we have for two years requested signing but so far without success.

You descend from Penare Point to walk behind the ruins of Portgiskey, crossing three stiles and a stepping stoned muddy section. Then do not bear left up the hill or turn right over the next stile but proceed curving right up the hill. As you come up the hill from Portgiskey keep with the hedge on your right to cross a stile just before the road, here turn right.

You come out on to the road close to the entrance of a massive caravan park, bear left a few yards to the main road B2373, signposted St Austell, and turn right. Turn first right again signposted Pentewan and called 'West End'.

Do not leave Pentewan unrefreshed, you have a long tough section ahead.

Turn right off the road into the harbour area just after the public toilets, walk along the harbour to the end of the cottages where you will see a path on your left going up through gardens to link up with the coast path behind the cottages. This path is frequently unsigned and does not look like a public right of way, but it is, and Cornish Ramblers fought a noble action to secure it, so please use it!

Back on the coast path put this book away, you will need your energies for other things! However take it out again when you have crossed a sloping bridge in a sizable wood.

Having crossed the bridge, you soon cross another small stream and come to a T junction. The right turn will take you down to Hallane Mill Beach, a lovely spot for a picnic with a waterfall. The coast path turns left soon to turn right again to start ascending to Black Head, a superb diversionary viewpoint on a clear day. It was once a rifle range but was purchased by N.T. helped in a small way with a donation from our Association.

The passage of the wood behind Ropehaven can give trouble if signing is not maintained. On entering the wood you turn right then left at the seat. Avoid right fork down to a cottage and turn sharp left at the top into a narrow walled lane. Turn right on to the narrow road. The path leaves it into a field just beyond the little car park/lay by.

At Porthpean Beach you go down on to the promenade to walk along past toilets and seasonal cafe. Continue to the end, it does not look likely, but there is a steep set of steps at the end to get you back on track once again.

Just before Charlestown is a stile through a high wall, disregard it and continue outside wall.

Grading: Easy   Distance-   6   579   4   360

See also our Mevagissey to Fowey Path Description

The official path does not go across the dock gate at the mouth of the harbour but provided the gate is closed most people will go that way.

You come up from the harbour keeping to the right of a house called Salamander. It is at first a tarmac track and then goes into fields. Later you come out beside a road, walk a few yards along it to turn right and then fork left.

After passing a big hotel you come out by a car park area, keep to the right of this to cross road and continue alongside a golf course.

You become more and more threatened by the clay processing industrial complex ahead, however continue bravely swinging finally left just before a wall/wire netting fence. The next bit could be called different, or interesting, but it is hardly beautiful! Avoid in a moment of panic the escape route left under a low railway culvert but continue ahead along what looks like a dead end to the road.

Go under a railway bridge to turn first right signposted A3082 Fowey, cross a level crossing and under another railway bridge. Proceed up a no entry with the Cornish Arms on your left, if you look up on the pub you will see you are walking along a street called Par Green. You pass The Good Shepherd Church on your right and Welcome Home Inn on your left. You then take second path off on the right – still not way marked despite three requests. To try and make this clearer, beginning of path has low concrete wall and house on right. It has a shrubby growth of buddleias and gorse and a house on the left. It soon comes to a tidal stream, swing left to walk along it, cross a road and come out in a caravan site, keep down the right hand side, to turn left and go along in front of a blue roofed building. You pass a cafe, which claims to be open all the year round, and finally come to Polmear with its seasonal cafe.

Do not fret if you miss all this you can simply walk along Par Green bear right at its end to get to Polmear by main road. It is less pleasant, gives less chance of refreshment but it gets you there just the same.

NTG – The trail described through Par is correct, the map is wrong.

51	**Par to Fowey**		**OS 204 (T) Par (B. Rail)**		

Grading: Moderate	Distance-	10	589	6	366

See also our Mevagissey to Fowey Path Description

It is a fine walk out from Polmear via Polkerris around the Gribbin Head to Menabilly and so on to Fowey. The availability of public transport from Par to Fowey makes this a very practical half day excursion with lovely views nearly all the way.

The path leaves the main road at Polmear just beside the eye-catching Rashleigh Cottages. For a very short while it is also The Saint's Way see note below*. At the first junction keep right and at the second turn right leaving the Saints to their own devices.

As you enter Polkerris you turn right, there is a sign but there is a grit bin in front of it. You go down to the beach and turn left, currently no sign, to proceed up ramp and join a path.

You should have no problem then until you enter the N.T. The Gribbin property through a field gate. There is soon a junction, go right and you come to a pedestrian gate. The official route goes to the Daymark and then sets off downhill inland. There is a better alternative seaward, keep ahead from the pedestrian gate to presently go through a second pedestrian gate and the way forward is then obvious passing through a little wood, when you come out proceed downhill to join the official route. If you want the best route but also wish to make a closer examination of the Daymark itself and to find out when it was built and why, and, should you wish to damage it, what it will cost you, turn left and go and find out. When you have satisfied your curiosity proceed due south and you will come to the second gate already mentioned.

You come down towards Polridmouth Beach and swing around close behind it, the path becomes concrete and there are even concrete stepping stones, this does not sound delightful but this is a lovely little stretch by the house and lake. The path goes steeply up swinging right through woods at the other side.

Again there should be no navigational problems until you reach Allday's Fields, you will see the memorial stone on your left. You enter a wood, first right is a loop path out towards the castle and there is a steep path dropping to the beach which can be used as a short cut when the tide is out. On entering the wood the more direct route is to go ahead at the first junction and to turn left at the next. This takes you down an increasingly rock cut lane which has a very sharp elbow about two thirds of the way down.

The path comes out at Readymoney Cove and it is then all road to Fowey. However if you are going straight on, watch for the ferry point on your right before you get into the town. It is down steps just after a hotel's tea garden.

*The Saints Way is a long distance footpath from Fowey to Padstow and a guide book is available. Quite apart from being a walk in its own right this could make a link enabling walkers to undertake a circular Cornish peninsula walk of approximately 220 miles.

52	Fowey to Polperro	OS 200 & 201 (T) Fowey (V) Polruan

Grading: Strenuous

Distance-	11	600	7	373

See also our Fowey to Looe Path Description

Leaving Fowey, if you have time on your side, you can go via the higher vehicular ferry to Bodinnick and walk the Halls Walk to Polruan. The more direct route already mentioned is the lower passenger ferry. This section is very good value for money in two senses of the word. Firstly there is a fine path all the way from Polruan to Polperro with magnificent sea views. Secondly, it is probably the toughest stretch of walking on the South Cornwall coast, those who have battled with us from Minehead may wonder what all the fuss is about, but someone unused to coastal walking may well find it takes some exertion.

Fowey/Polruan (River Fowey)
Polruan Ferry Co. Ltd
Tomsyard
East Street
Polruan-by-Fowey
Cornwall
PL23 1PB
Tel: 01726 832626

All the year round. Continuous. Summer, Easter to mid October: From Town Quay, Fowey. 0715 to 2300 hrs (2330 during August). Winter, mid October–Easter: From Whitehouse Slip, Fowey. Oct/Mar 0715 to 1900 hrs. Sundays: 1000 to 1700 hrs. No service Christmas Day, limited service Boxing and New Years Day.

In winter months when the weather deteriorates you may find that the ferry operates to and from the town quay at Fowey rather than the jetty lower down the harbour. There should be sign up to this effect.

Landing from the ferry go along the quay and up the steps just beside The Lugger, at the top turn right along West Street (believe it or not!) and then left when you get to Battery Lane. The path comes out in a grassy area, keep with the wall on your left going round the corner. The path goes right, just after an earth bank and then proceed ahead across another open area with a small ruin up on your left. It joins the road beside a school, continue ahead to turn sharp right just before the notice saying 'Furze Park'.

About two miles after leaving Polruan there is a considerable hill behind Great Lantic Beach. If short of exercise you can go all the way to the top and turn right there. The route we recommend turns right about 30 yards from the top go over a stile to drop down again. Ignore the first two turnings right they are beach paths. Presently a wide path joins from left. Shortly after that there is another path right this is a spectacular, even more seaward, route.

Although a definitive right of way is shown below the Watch House, at the moment the practical route is the broad path above it. Assuming you are on this path, ignore the stile on your right which goes directly to the house. Just after this is another loop path right but it has little in views to compensate for the extra effort.

When you come to Lansallos Cove, look for West Combe on your map, a sign points you inland for the Coast Path. Unless the tide is fully in, it is more interesting to go ahead and turn right down to the beach through a small rock cut lane. Go left, cross the back of the beach and climb the little rock cut steps on the other side.

Later you enter the N.T. Chapel Cliff property and there are a series of parallel paths all going to Polperro so if you miss out or cannot fathom our instructions below, do not worry just keep going east. Having said that, this is the best way; you enter the property and then climb, at the top at first junction keep right. At the second junction keep left, the right is a beach path only. There are then several paths off left but you are looking for a path going right some way ahead. When you get to the junction you want, a seat is visible ahead on the wrong path and three houses far ahead. After you have turned right at this junction there is another little path right and then another bigger one; ignore both going forward to a large open rocky area beyond a shelter. From the rocky area turn left and the official route into Polperro is the first set of steps on the right.

Grading: Moderate Distance- 8 608 5 378

See also our Fowey to Looe Path Description

This next section is particularly well walked and the local bus company is sufficiently commercially minded to put up bus times for cliff walkers between Polperro and Looe actually on the path!

In Polperro you have to walk behind the harbour crossing Roman Bridge to turn right. Leaving Polperro there is a loop path right called Reuben's Walk. If you take this turn left again just before the miniature lighthouse.

Note the spectacularly sited War Memorial on Downend Point. A little way past this is another beach path right which ignore.

At the time of writing there is a landfall and diversion inland just before Talland Beach. However we hope this problem will be overcome soon. At the beach there are refreshments in season and we recommend the cafe to all but faint hearted walkers who may have thought the coast path long. The reason for this is, that inside, they can learn about a ten year old walking all the way from Land's End to John O'Groats!

After the cafe go up the tarmac turn left past the toilets and then right. After about a quarter of a mile turn right into a car park and so back on the path again.

Entering Looe you have a long stretch along the seafront but presently come to a stretch of road with no pavement. This drops into a dip and watch for a battlemented look-out platform on your right. Just past this are steps down to the harbour area of the river, that is the best way to go. This has a double advantage it keeps you away from the traffic and takes you past the long seasonal ferry to East Looe, certainly if you are walking straight through this is the best way to go.

Grading: Moderate Distance- 12 620 8 386

See also our Looe to Plymouth Path Description

This is a section with several difficulties. You leave East Looe by turning up Castle Street, cross a minor cross roads continuing up the hill. The road peters out becoming a pleasant high level path above the sea.

The path becomes a road again and at first junction bear right. Pass Bodrigy a seasonal cafe, continue on the road until just after it has swung right. Here a steep tarmac path takes off right just beyond a big electric cable post, the house on left is called 'Skewys'.

At the top of the path you come to a road again to continue ahead for a while until the road swings left but the path goes forward again between houses. Go down steps, do not turn left or right but continue nearly opposite to go ahead.

The path comes down to Millendreath (seasonal refreshments) pass behind the beach to go up the cul-de-sac road the other side. The road becomes a path in a sunken lane but shortly after you reach road again turn right into the Bodigga Cliff N.T. property.

The path is now greatly improved and you should enjoy this stretch. However be careful part way through is a left fork and shortly after a right fork which need to be avoided, for two years we have asked for signing here without effect.

The path comes out on the road above Seaton, turn right down what is Looe Hill. Go down to the bottom and turn right into Bridge Road, if time presses the quickest route is along the road, however at most states of the tide there is a better alternative. Where the road starts to go uphill, opposite the Post Office, there is a wall on the seaward side. Behind this wall is the beginning of coastal defence works with a path on top. After a while you have to go down to the beach and then you have two choices. If you turn inland at the first stream you will arrive at the centre of Downderry, shops, seasonal refreshment etc. If you do not want to do this but wish to minimize road walking, and there is a lot in the next section to come, go on to the second stream and turn left there. You come up beside a school to turn right along a road.

Continue with the road until it sweeps inland at a hairpin bend. The path takes off right here, next to a house named 'Downderry Lodge', zig-zagging uphill to come eventually into a field. The coast path should then go right and many people have mistakenly done that finding it hard to believe that over twenty years after the Cornish section of the Coast Path was opened it is still unfinished! However the dull by pass route goes forward through a few inland fields and then joins a road where turn right. You then have a long tedious section on the road before turning right again just after a bungalow named 'The Bungalow' to go down to Portwrinkle to turn left.

BMG – Page 76. Third line from bottom – for 'left' read 'right'.

| 55 | Portwrinkle to Cremyll (for Plymouth) | (V) Cawsand/Kingsand |

Grading: Moderate   Distance-   **21   641   13   399**

See also our Looe to Plymouth Path Description

If the tide is out and there is no firing at Tregantle Fort, you can in fact walk along the beach the whole way to Polhawn Cove and some find this a better alternative to what is currently offered. If you do this you need the first path down right to the beach and be warned, the last mile before Polhawn becomes rocky.

The current route takes the second path on the right going up opposite to the entrance to the golf club. It is currently well marked except right at the end of the course, where you need to aim for the pedestrian gate seen on top of a rise.

You come out to the road but the path for a while is just inside the hedge. This travesty of a path ends by the road junction to Torpoint where you have to come down to the road and turn right along it. All this agony is caused by some bureaucrat in M.O.D. who refuses to let you walk through the rifle range when not in use, if it can be done elsewhere, even on a tank firing range in Dorset, with good will it could here.

However back to the road, you pass Tregantle Fort entrance, the road swings left and shortly you turn right signposted Whitsand Bay etc. The road swings right shortly with N.T. properties on your right, they have promised paths here so watch for them but at last visit none were visible.

There is another long stretch of road, until you see notices for Whitsand Bay Holiday Park on the left and the Coast Path starts again on the right, at this point even sharper right is a seasonal cafe. The coast path is now well marked and a great improvement over the road, but it does descend and climb twice. So if time presses you can stay on the road until you see on left Wiggle Old Farm House, turn right there and within a few yards you will pick up the Coast Path again.

The path is then clear until you are immediately inland of Rame Head, a diversion out well worth making if conditions are clear. The path then proceeds across an unmarked junction, go straight ahead, along a good high level path above the sea, when you get to the road keep right.

Continue along tarmac avoiding path turn off on right, the road turns left with intermittent views ahead to Plymouth Sound Breakwater and presently over a quarter of a mile later, takes off into the wood right.

Traversing Cawsand/Kingsand the official and in fact easiest way is not straightforward and only some of it is signposted, so read the next paragraph carefully.

You enter Cawsand from 'Pier Lane', go across the square to pick up 'Garrett St'. As you come towards the end of this street look for the old Devon/Corn boundary mark on a house on your right. Then turn right in front of the post office. Soon you will approach a street called 'The Cleave'. Just before you reach it turn left. Then turn first right up what is 'Heavitree Road'but they do not help you by telling you that until you are a few yards up it. As you ascend you will presently see 'Lower Row' on your left, here turn right and enter Mount Edgcumbe Country Park.

When you come out on to a road at Hooe Lodge turn right but look, in only a very few yards, for the path leaving the road on the left. You continue along a section of the one time Earl's Drive but shortly after going under an old stone arch turn right. Follow the signs which direct you down to the foreshore for a very few yards but you soon go up again.

You continue through a high deer gate, you come out by a classical summer house keep along right to pick up a concrete driveway, and later right again when drive goes left to walk inside of a hedge. You pass an old blockhouse on your left, note inscription on second side.

The path comes out by The Orangery (seasonal cafe), go through an arch go forward to turn right through the park gates to the ferry point for Plymouth.

BMG – Page 79. Most of that road route is now off it.

56 | Cremyll (for Plymouth) to Turnchapel OS 201 (T) Plymouth (B.Rail)

| Grading: Easy | Distance- | 11 | 652 | 7 | 406 |

See also our Plymouth to Wembury Path Description

The distance for this section is from the River Tamar to Warren Point, Wembury via the Plymouth (Sutton Harbour) to Turnchapel ferry or water taxi.

Cremyll/Plymouth
Cremyll Ferry,
Cremyll Quay,
Cremyll,
Nr. Torpoint,
Cornwall.
Tel: 01752 822105.

All year round at intervals of ¹/₂ hr to 1 hr. Summer service from 1 May to 18 September: From Mt. Edgcumbe 0650 to 2015. From Plymouth 0720 to 2030 weekdays. Saturdays from Mt. Edgcumbe 0815 to 2100 and from Plymouth 0845 to 2115. Sundays from Mt. Edgcumbe 0900 to 2100 and from Plymouth 2115. Winter service from 19 September to 30 April: There are fewer ferries and on weekdays the last ferry leaves Mt. Edgcumbe at 1815 and Plymouth at 1830, Saturdays 1830 and 1845, Sundays 1700 and 1715. Sunday ferries commence at 0900 and 0915.

On landing at Admirals Hard walk up the road and turn right into Cremyll Street, and continue to the massive gates of King William Yard. Pass them on your right and continue on out to Firestone Bay. At the sea wall you have a fine view to Drake's Island and beyond towards Wembury. A slight excursion could be made by turning right to walk out to Western King's Point and Devil's Point, for River Tamar views. You will have to return. From the sea wall you walk into Durnford Street, continue along it until you arrive at a church on your right, where you turn right. This short road brings you into Admiralty Street, turn left and you will soon come upon the large gates of Millbay Docks. You can walk through the docks along North Quay passing the large Brittany Ferries complex. If the gates are closed and/or guarded, thus denying access, return to Durnford Street. Turn right and walk past the Royal Marine Barracks, turning right immediately after them. This will bring you into Millbay Road where you continue on to the Dock Gates (east).

If you are lucky enough to gain access to North Quay, however, you may be luckier still and the Inner Basin could present you with the sounds, sights and activities of preparation for some long-distance yacht race.

At the corner of North and East Quays, turn right and then look for an exit from the docks into Millbay Road, where you turn right and then right again into West Hoe Road. Keep to this road passing the ex-British Telecom House. You are now in the West Hoe area and the streets surrounding you have numerous B & B establishments.

As you approach a terrace of tall houses, mainly small hotels, watch out for a path on your right known as Rusty Anchor. This is a slight diversion from the main road and provides a shoreline walk.

On regaining the main road, turn right and continue along the Hoe foreshore. You stay on this promenade all the way around to The Barbican and Sutton Harbour. But, you could achieve grand views over Plymouth Sound by climbing steps opposite the swimming pool up to the lighthouse, Smeaton's Tower, and passing that to cross The Hoe to have a look at Sir Francis Drake, still scanning the English Channel for the Armada.

Retrace your steps and continue your shore-line walk to The Barbican. A small jetty on your right is of historic significance in that it is the site of the Mayflower Steps, of great interest to our US members.

Whatever you decide upon, ferry or the walking route, it is well worth exploring the ancient Barbican area before carrying on.

Plymouth to Turnchapel Ferry and Water Taxi Service

From Sutton Harbour the ferry will operate a fixed schedule winter and summer. Outside that schedule it will operate as a water taxi anywhere – Kingsand, Cremyll, Sutton Harbour, Turnchapel and Fort Bovisand. (Mobile 'phone – 0585 138371).

Clovelly Bay Company Limited
The Quay, Turnchapel,
Plymouth PL9 9TF
Telephone: 01752 404231

Walking Route – Sutton Harbour to Turnchapel

Lock gates have now been installed at Sutton Harbour so walk on across them into Teat's Hill Road. As you progress along Teat's Hill Road you will arrive at the Breakwater Inn. Turn right here, but do not walk into the scrap yard unless you want to view vehicles being broken up.

Pass the scrap yard on your right and you will see an overgrown Breakwater Hill, fringed with scrap cars. Carry on up the hill for a limestone, clifftop walk with views over the Cattewater. At a fork in the lane bear left and you will descend to the area of Cattedown Wharf. We will now just supply directions – continue on past warehouses into Maxwell Road, turn left at Oakfield Terrace Road, turn right at Elliott Road, and turn right at Cattewater Road. Within a few hundred yards you will find an extremely busy dual carriageway on your left with traffic flowing towards the City Centre. Join this road and walk against the stream of traffic across Laira Bridge over the River Plym. You have pavements to walk upon. At the first roundabout turn right into Oreston Road.

You now have a choice:-

(a) Across a piece of grass on your left you will find an old railway line which is now a cycle/walk route through to Radford Lake or,

(b) Keep on to the top of the road, bear right, then when you reach Rollis Park Road, turn right to descend to Oreston Quay. You are beside the water only for a couple of hundred yards, and at Plymstock Road turn left. Start climbing away from the estuary and at Lower Saltram turn right and carry straight on to Radford Lake.

The 'castle' through which you walk was once the lodge to a large house, now no more. Turning right after the causeway brings you to a path alongside the southern shore of Hooe Lake. At the time of writing it was not waymarked, but you should not go far wrong if you keep to this path. You will join a narrow road which leads to Hooe Lake Road.

Walk straight across the grassy area keeping to the shore and turn right along Barton Road, and by staying with this road you will come into Turnchapel.

BMG – Does not cover any of the walk from the River Tamar to Heybrook Bay. We think you ought to walk it all, especially Plymouth Hoe and the Barbican area.

NTG – Also does not supply walking instructions for this 7 miles of the coast path.

---

57 | Turnchapel to Wembury (Warren Point) | OS 201

Grading: Easy	Distance-	11	663	7	413

See also our Plymouth to Wembury Path Description

This section is well worth walking as a circular day's walk which may be accomplished by catching a bus from Plymouth to Turnchapel and walking to Wembury or vice versa, bus to Knighton and walking back to Turnchapel.

For the ongoing coast path walker the start is at Turnchapel where there is an immediate climb up St Johns Road. You will pass gates that once were the entrance to RAF Mountbatten. It is hoped that by the time we print the next edition of this guide we will be able to describe a new shoreline coast path, as the City of Plymouth has plans for the whole area.

Passing the gates take the next road on the right which will lead you past the entrance to Staddon Fort which is another establishment that was abandoned by the MOD many many years ago than the RAF did at Mountbatten. Watch out for an exit from the road on the right. You will walk along a grassy area with views all round. Return to the road again for a gentle ascent. In a wooded area you will find the coast path on the right which is a straightforward walk to Bovisand, another of the great forts that once defended Plymouth

On the descent from the harbour the path can be seen ahead between hundreds of chalet/huts and the sea. At Heybrook Bay watch out for the coast path – turn off from the road after the last house.

The path passes in front of the guns of HMS Cambridge. When firing is taking place you will certainly hear it. Red flags fly during the shooting and when it is about to commence. Do not walk seaward of them but follow a well marked diversion to the left. This path circles the property of the Royal Navy and will return the walker to the coast safely. Needless to say, if the red flags are not flying then the official coast path is yours but do not loiter along the section.

There is a free telephone – 0800 833608 for prior information of firing times. Firing usually takes place between 0900 and 1800, rarely at night or at weekends and Bank Holidays. The gunnery school is closed at Christmas, Easter and for three weeks in August.

Now follows a low cliff top walk to Wembury Beach. The path passes seaward of the church and climbs to a level path that leads into the estuary of the River Yealm. At a small house, The Rocket House, once used for the storage of life saving apparatus, the official path takes off downhill diagonally towards the river and the ferry point. We suggest you walk down to the ferry point even if the ferry is not running or you do not intend to use it because you can take advantage of a scenic short circular back to the Rocket House. Once the ferry steps have been reached carry on for a few yards then take a path on the left that climbs to good views over Newton Ferrers and Noss Mayo.

AFG – The inland alternative is around HMS Cambridge, not through it.

| 58 | Wembury (Warren Point) to Bigbury on Sea | OS 201 & 202 |

| Grading: Starts easy but becomes strenuous | Distance- | 22 | 685 | 14 | 427 |

See also our Wembury (Warren Point) to Bigbury on Sea Path Description

The first obstacle is crossing the River Yealm.

Wembury (Warren Point) to Noss Mayo Ferry.
River Yealm

Bill Gregor,	Seasonal, all week.
15 The Fairway,	10 to 22 April.
Newton Ferrers,	22 May to 2 Sept.
PL8 1DW.	1000–1100 and 1500–1600.
01752 872318.	

The ferryman is often there outside these hours. Stop at steps at Warren Point or slipway at Noss Mayo. Look towards Newton Ferrers and shout "Ferry" and wave. We suggest you might also telephone ahead to Mr. Gregor to give him an idea of your ETA.

If there is no ferry then this means a walk back to the Rocket House to follow the lane into Knighton. There is an hourly bus service (number 48) to Plymstock and Plymouth where there is available an infrequent service to Noss Mayo (number 94). For a quicker conveyance around the estuary there are reasonably priced taxis available:-

Wembury Cabs – John Pitcher (01752 862151) and
Tims Taxis – Tim Craig (01752 830225)

From the Rocket House the track leads into a road. At Wembury House a stile leads to a field and to the footpath junction. The path you want is the one to the right which runs alongside a high wall. Follow it to the end of the wall where it goes through two successive kissing gates. It then bears left approximately 330° across fields towards Knighton. As you leave the fields it goes down a few steps. Turn left and then first right. This will bring you out onto the road. Turn left and the bus stop is a little further along on the other side of the road just before the pub. The distance from ferry point to bus stop is 1¹/₂ miles.

Before reaching the bus stop you will pass a telephone box where you can call a taxi if you want.

For those who contemplate walking around the estuary please take care as the A379 is a very busy road. We have asked the Countryside Commission to start thinking about the installation of a riverside walk around, so in the not too distant future we may get to write a description of how to do it.

At Noss Mayo those who have come around will have a picturesque riverside walk out to where those who have been fortunate enough with the ferry will disembark. The well marked path climbs through woodlands to pick up Lord Revelstoke's nine-mile drive made for the carriages of his guests at Membland Hall, since demolished.

There is a definitive path loop seaward as you approach Stoke Beach. Use this if you wish to visit the historic Church of St Peter the Poor Fisherman. This will mean an uphill road walk to regain the coast path. If you do not divert then the path crosses the Stoke Beach road to continue along, passing the ruined 'Tea House'.

You are now in for a very steep descent then a climb up to St Anchorites Rock and you pass Bugle Hole. The section then to Mothecombe Beach provides superb views to the Erme estuary. It has been fairly described as England's most unspoilt river estuary. We certainly believe it to be the most attractive.

River Erme   No ferry

Low water is at about the same time as the Devonport Tide Table shown here.

It is usually possible to wade the river 1 hour each side of low water along the old ford. Great care should be taken because heavy rains or seas can make the crossing dangerous. On modern maps the old ford is not shown but this in fact ran from Ordnance map ref. 614 476 to map ref. 620 478. In other words, the old ford connected the road by the row of coastguard cottages with the end of the inland road to Wonwell Beach from Kingston.

Should you arrive at the River Erme at a time that promises a very long wait for low tide to enable you to wade across then there is an inland alternative. This alternative is of about 7 miles with fairly steep up and down country lanes. You are the best judge of your rate of travel so the decision to wait for the tide or continue walking is yours.

If you follow the riverside paths shown on OS map 202 you will be trespassing on a private estate so follow the narrow country lanes to Holbeton village. Then continue on a northerly route to Ford and Hole Farm. Soon after passing Hole Farm take off on a public footpath on your right. From here to the main A379 road is about 3/4 mile. Turn right to cross the River Erme at Sequer's Bridge. Stay on the A379 for about 1/2 mile but take care as this is an extremely busy road. You will see a road on your right signposted to Orcheston. Follow this road south towards the village of Kingston but before you reach that village you will see road signs to Wonwell Beach. Just before the slipway on to the sands you have a choice. If the tide now permits you can continue south along the beach or take to the waymarked coast path in the woodlands on your left. We think this preferable because of the lovely views you will get of the Erme Estuary.

Beyond the Erme the walking becomes tougher but the all round views will compensate the effort. There is an interesting low tide alternative at Westcombe Beach. Go onto the beach for a walk through the promontory to Ayrmer Cove via one or other of two 15 yard long caves. You will walk on shingle through them but be a little careful on rocks that can be slippery once through the caves. This is a low tide diversion only.

The path passes Challaborough with its cafe and caravans to Bigbury on Sea.

Burgh Island can be visited by walking across the sands or by a 'sea tractor' if the tide is in. The pub is very old, the hotel is fascinating art deco modern and the hut at the top of the island stands on the site of a chapel. This hut was used by the 'huers' – pilchard fishermen on the lookout for shoals of fish.

BMG – Page 16. Go further upstream than shown on the map to wade the River Erme. Cross over towards the road on the east side. The woodland route is not shown from that road southwards.

---

59 | Bigbury on Sea to Hope Cove, Inner Hope   OS 202 (V) Bantham (V) Thurlestone

Grading: Moderate   Distance-   9   694   6   433

See also our Bigbury on Sea to Salcombe Path Description

There are riverside footpaths along both west and east banks of the River Avon to Aveton Gifford. This makes the inland walking route from Bigbury on Sea to Bantham and vice versa about 9 miles in total. The OS Landranger Series 2 maps show the riverside paths. What you have to watch is that the road between the two words 'Ford' is tidal and therefore is at times submerged.

The official route turns right at the bottom of the road on to what is called Clematon Hill at the western side of the mouth of the River Avon. There are good views here across the estuary but unfortunately you have to walk up the busy road to Mount Folly Farm afterwards. However, again there is compensation because the views southward across the estuary just after the farm are particularly spectacular.

Bigbury/Bantham (River Avon)	Seasonal. Not Sundays.
H Cater, Yorick, West Buckland	10–22 April
Kingsbridge, Devon	22 May to 2 Sept
Tel Kingsbridge (01548) 560593	1000–1100 and 1500–1600.

During busy periods and good weather Mr. Cater may be around outside these times. We suggest you telephone Mr Cater the day before you require the ferry and give him your estimated time of arrival. Low water is about the same time as the Devonport Tide Table. It is possible at low tide, when not rough, or the river is not in flood, to wade the river. However, we strongly stress we are not advising this as a cheap method of avoiding the ferry crossing. When the ferry is working, you are strongly advised to use it because wading is not easy and you may get a lot wetter than you expect. You will most likely be up to your thighs in water and in no circumstances should the crossing be attempted if conditions are wrong. The two guide points are just below the ferry crossing. On the true right bank – the western side – there is a well defined hedge running north and south with pine trees. On the left bank – the eastern side – there is a castellated building with battlements and a little flag pole in the middle. (This castle is just above the famous thatched boat house which is so well known from many pictures taken of the River Avon and Bantham.) However, if crossing from the true right to the left – in other words from west to east – take off at the hedge and wade towards the castle-like building. If going the other way, vice versa. Please note it is important that you do wade at this point. The river looks shallow in a number of other places but there are deeper channels and indeed soft sand patches which can make it extremely difficult. Further towards the sea, there is a considerable tidal ebb which can be exceedingly dangerous.

PLEASE NOTE WHEN THE FERRY IS NOT OPERATING A RECOMMENDED WAY TO REACH BANTHAM IS BY REASONABLY PRICED TAXIS:

Arrow Cars – Mr Kemp – (Telephone: 01548 856120) and

D & C Taxis (Telephone 01548 561560).

It should always be borne in mind that the depth of water at low tide and consequently safe passage across is affected by natural conditions inasmuch that strong south west or westerly winds tend to bank up water in the English Channel and that therefore, there will be a greater depth of water than expected. This will also happen if there is a lot of rain in the catchment areas of the rivers, with consequently more water coming down. Caution: although we know several who have waded the River Avon we do not recommend it; great care is required, especially by those with backpacks.

VERY IMPORTANT – PLEASE TAKE NOTE

AT DEAD LOW WATER WE STRESS THAT YOU MUST CONSIDER VERY SERIOUSLY WHETHER YOU SHOULD WADE THIS RIVER. IT IS VERY DIFFICULT AND CAN BE DANGEROUS EVEN FOR TALL AND STRONG ADULTS. MANY OF OUR MEMBERS, INCLUDING YOUR SECRETARY WILL NOT VENTURE ACROSS. THEIR OPINION BEING – "WHEN THE FERRY IS NOT RUNNING THEN THE **ONLY** ALTERNATIVE IS TO GO ROUND".

Inland Walking Route

When the tide is not low (and we urge you to read again our advice about wading) and the ferry is not available the only way to the other side is an inland walk to Aveton Gifford and around. This is a pleasant 7 mile (12 km) diversion as it is mostly along country paths. Walking through agricultural land in deep country makes a change from the coast. The paths are shown on OS Pathfinder map 1362 and are quite well marked but they are little used and are not always easy to follow. Allow plenty of time for some heavy walking, for straying off route or for a possible delay at the tidal road near Aveton Gifford.

Disregard the coast path where it turns right through Mount Folly Farm and descends to the ferry point, but proceed towards Bigbury for 60 yards to the next footpath sign. Turn right into the field over a stone stile and walk along the field edge. Over a wooden stile will bring you onto the golf course where, after a short distance, you meet a surfaced track. Turn left towards the clubhouse for two hundred yards where you turn right between two Nissen Huts going down a track to Hexdown Farm. Pass through the farm buildings and immediately turn half right as waymarked and continue downhill with the boundary on your left. Proceed along a track through a timber gate down to Villa Crusoe. Follow the footpath sign slightly left along a tarmac drive, into woodland, then through Lincombe and on to the B3392 on a corner. Proceed northwards towards Bigbury for 350 yards (be careful of the traffic) and turn right at the footpath sign to Aveton Gifford (via tidal road). Cross the field to a post and wire fence and enter the top of Doctors Wood. Re-emerge into a field and cross due east to a wooden stile. Proceed along a high level path (beautiful views) then walk downhill to the tidal road which will bring you to Aveton Gifford. There is a viable alternative if the tide is over the road by walking north-westward to Foxhole then north-eastward to Waterhead and Aveton Gifford. The whole path is adequately waymarked.

Cross the Avon on the roadbridge (A379) towards Kingsbridge, and turn right at the end of the bridge into a cul-de-sac. Continue to a gate at a signpost, and straight on to a metalled road, where you turn right at a signpost.

Bear left at road fork, following the footpath sign to a gate; turn right here and follow a fence on the right, and through another gate into a field.

Turn half right down to the bottom of the valley, and bear right to a gate with a waymark "to Stiddicombe Creek'. Cross this as best you can (not easy) and enter wood on right. Work steadily uphill to top corner and follow waymark signs along the top of the field with a hedge on the left (watch out for herons by the river) to a stile by a gate; over another stile and continue. Bear right and cross a farm track to a gate between walls. Cross the stream ahead with stepping stones, and along to a stile and waymark signs, where you turn right and straight on to Bantham, where you turn right and through the village where you will see the ferry sign. Here you would have stepped ashore had it been operating. The coast path is straight on towards the sea.

Some of this walk is shown in the National Trail Guide.

There were recent problems at Thurlestone Golf Course but these have been resolved and the path is happily back on the coast once more. However, you should take great care where the path proceeds along the seaward boundary of the Thurlestone Golf Course, watching out for golfers and where they hit the ball. We have had a report of a walker on this section who was hit in the mouth by a golf ball at close range with resulting horrific damage to teeth and lips.

| **60** | **Hope Cove, Inner Hope to Salcombe Ferry** | **OS 202 V Hope Cove** |

Grading: Strenuous   Distance-   **12**   **706**   **7**   **440**

See also our Bigbury on Sea to Salcombe Path Description

Excellent coastal walking, some of the finest in South Devon. This section also makes an easily accomplished day walk from Kingsbridge or Marlborough using Hope and Salcombe buses.

Before leaving Inner Hope one ought to walk along the inland road to look at 'The Square' and its attractive thatched cottages. To return to the coast path. It is well marked out to Bolt Tail where the remains of an Iron Age fort is marked by a dry stone wall and the remains of a ditch.

The path is obvious to Bolberry Down and on to a viewpoint overlooking Soar Mill Cove. There is a steep descent to the cove but the climb out is easier. We have heard of walkers going wrong as they near the rocky splendid Bolt Head. The correct route is the coast route, do not divert inland anywhere until the headland is reached. The path then runs due north into and around Starehole Bay. Here, in 1936 the grain clipper Herzogovin Cecille finally sank, having struck the Ham Stone off Soar Mill Cove.

From the bay the path joins the Courtenay Way which was cut out under rocky pinnacles. The way ahead is through woodlands to the roadway below the National Trust's Overbecks House and Youth Hostel. Follow the road to South Sands where, in season, a ferry can be taken to the main ferry point in Salcombe. If it is not running or you are a purist the way ahead to the town and ferry for East Portlemouth is along the most seaward roads ahead.

AFG – Incorrect route shown between Soar Mill Cove and Bolt Head.

BMG – Incorrect route shown between Soar Mill Cove and Off Cove.

Grading: Strenuous   Distance-   20   726   13   453

See also our Salcombe to Torcross Path Description

This is first class walking, some of the best of the whole coast path.

Salcombe to East Portlemouth Ferry	All year round Nov–March.
The Salcombe Ferry,	0800 to 1700 hrs half-hourly. April–October
North Lodge,	continuous service running to 1930 hrs. July
Landmark Road,	and August Sundays, Saturdays and
Salcombe,	Bank Holidays 0830 hrs start.
Devon TQ8 8NY	
Tel: (01548) 842061/842364	

Having crossed the estuary the path goes off to the right along the narrow road. Just after the National Trust car park at Mill Bay there is a choice of paths. One goes uphill on the left through trees, but we suggest you stay with the lower one to the right which is, after all, the official path. It is a pleasant walk along Rickham Common and passes below the Gara Rock Hotel (refreshments available).

After Gammon Head a look towards Prawle Point will reveal the wreck of the Demetrios which was smashed onto the cliff in December 1992 when she broke her tow en route to the breakers yard.

It is recommended that you walk to the very end of Prawle Point, to the Coastguard lookout. The official route is back inland again but near to the lookout on the east side of the point is a path descending a valley. This is the better one. Prawle Point is National Trust property and there is a true coast path along the top of low cliffs around Copstone Cove to link in with the official route at Western Cove.

It is easy walking for a while along the edges of fields on what is a 'raised' beach. The path then becomes rocky and up and down prior to Lanacombe Beach. The path is straightforward to Start Point and on to Torcross but we do advise leaving yourself time to make the diversion to the old deserted village at Hall Sands. Very few who go down there to see the ruins alongside the sea will not be moved by the experience.

There have been cliff falls between Hall Sands and Torcross but the authorities have made sensible slight adjustments.

NTG – Page 110 paragraph 5. The accommodation is only self-catering apartments.

Grading: Moderate   Distance –   16   742   10   463

The coast path runs along the length of the shingle bank. You can walk either side of the road, the top of the beach for sea views or alongside the Ley for bird watching.

There is no coast path from Strete Gate to Warren Cove except a few yards of road at Blackpool Sands. Whilst we await, yet another year, news of an improved route you have to walk Devon County Council's apology for a coast path to Warren Cove. Follow their waymarks. It is a reasonable country walk but it sure is no coast path.

Thanks to the fund raising efforts of the Women's Institute the National Trust now own the rest of this section from Warren Cove. Dartmouth Castle commands the river mouth and, time permitting, should be visited.

In season there is a regular ferry from the Castle to Dartmouth. You could enjoy a beautiful boat trip instead of walking the road. If the road is your way ahead then as you near the town centre watch out for steps on the right leading down to Bayard's Cove and Wharf, used often in films of old seafaring days.

NTG – Page 117 (map). No Youth Hostel at Strete now.

BMG – The route shown between Strete Gate and Stoke Fleming is not the official one –

see NTG. Anyway, this poor route could be altered soon by Devon County Council. Hopefully, for an improved one but we are not optimistic.

BMG – The better route to Dartmouth Castle is not shown.

63	**Dartmouth to Brixham**		**OS 202 (T) Dartmouth (V) Kingswear**		

Grading: Strenuous	Distance-	18	760	11	474

See also our Dartmouth to Brixham Path Description

Walkers will probably use the lower ferry to cross the River Dart but there are two other regular ferries which also run all year round. Nearby is the passenger ferry, which lands by the steam railway station, and which gives a more comfortable crossing, and if these two are not running then further up the river is the higher ferry taking pedestrians and vehicles. If you use the higher ferry you will then need to turn right along the railway line to the road, then turn right again and descend the hill to join the coastal path by the lower ferry slipway.

Dartmouth/Kingswear
South Hams District Council, Lower Ferry,
Lower Ferry Office, The Square,
Kingswear TQ6 0AA
Tel: (01803) 752342

0700/2255 hrs Sunday start 0800 hrs.
Winter – 15 minutes service,
Summer – 6 minutes service.
Last ferry leaves: Dartmouth 2255 hrs,
Kingswear 2245 hrs.

On landing at Kingswear, by the lower ferry, pass through an arch (there is a signpost but it is in a shop window and may be missed) ascend Alma Steps then turn right along Beacon Road. In 1¹/4 miles turn right down steps at Warren Woods where this section of the path is on the estate which was owned by the late Col. H. Jones the Falkland Islands V.C. and has very properly been dedicated to his memory.

When you reach the old Battery Buildings at Froward Point do divert inland to see 'The Daymark' navigation tower nearby if time permits but then return to the coast path to continue. The sign here is 8³/4 miles to Brixham and the path descends steeply going right from the back corner of the derelict look out building and then passes through the World War II gun and searchlight positions. Next at Pudcombe Cove you can obtain access to the National Trust gardens at Coleton Fishacre if they are open.

Now a pleasant walk to Berry Head Country Park, a Nature Reserve with much of interest – do spend time here if you can. The Northern Fort, one of the two Napoleonic Forts contains the Berry Head lighthouse and the old guardhouse is now a cafe, open in the season and sometimes out of season as well.

Having left Berry Head and descending Berry Head Road, when you are level with the Breakwater descend the steps to the new promenade which follows the water's edge past the new marina to the inner harbour.

64	**Brixham to Torquay Harbour**		**OS 202 (T) Brixham (T) Paignton**		

Grading: Moderate	Distance-	13	773	8	482

See also our Brixham to Shaldon Path Description

Distances are taken along the official path where there is one, then along the back of Goodrington Sands beach, around Roundham Head, along Paignton and Preston sea fronts and along the promenade at Torquay.

From Brixham to Elbury Cove the path is fair though not as scenic as one might hope. Thereafter it becomes more urbanised with the poorest section from Hollicombe to Torquay Harbour where you usually have quite heavy traffic nearby. Remember, in case of need, there is a very frequent bus service from Brixham to Torquay via Paignton! There is, also, a regular Brixham/Torquay ferry service.

When departing from Brixham leave by the new path running along the harbour, signposted

Coastal Footpath to Oxen Cove and Freshwater Car Park. At the car park continue on past the Zeneca Brixham Environmental Laboratory and on to the Battery Gardens where you follow the lower path to Fishcombe Cove. Ascend from the cove and at the road junction turn right, signpost Public Footpath to Churston Ferrers.

At the far end of Elbury Cove ignore the more obvious path going inland and leave the beach by ascending the steps. Take care at Broadsands beach that you do not follow the path up the cliff at the eastern end, but turn left up the road, pass under the railway bridge and then turn immediately right where the coast path is signposted.

At Goodrington follow the promenade round and just before the end a zig-zag path takes you up to Roundham Head.

At Hollicombe Head you can turn right and go through the delightful park that was once the gas works. Bear left to emerge through the main gate onto the road. Then turn right for Torquay.

CP – Between Broadsands and Goodrington the path crosses back under the railway line. There is no road walking until Paignton Harbour.

NTG – Page 133. Do not use Overgang. Look out for new coast path.

NTG – Broadsands – stay with the sea wall until well past halfway.

BMG – Does not cover Brixham to Babbacombe. Over ten miles omitted!

| 65 | **Torquay Harbour to Shaldon** | **OS 202 (T) Torquay (B.Rail)** |

Grading: Strenuous   Distance-   17   790   11   493

See also our Brixham to Shaldon Path Description

You walk on round Torquay Inner Harbour, turning left up Beacon Hill and soon reach The Imperial Hotel where you will find there are now new signposts on each side of the road entrance, Coast Path Daddyhole Plain. Turn in right here to pass in front of the main entrance to the hotel and then follow the scenic path to the grassy plateau of Daddyhole Plain, which you cross to find the path descending to Meadfoot Beach.

At the far end of Meadfoot Beach turn right through a small car park and ascend to Marine Drive where turn right. Shortly turn right at a signpost Thatcher Point and follow the track which rejoins the road further up. Here the route follows a path above the left hand side of the road and at the end cross the road and take the Bishops Walk path signposted Ansteys Cove.

On the road by the car park above Ansteys Cove you can, time and energy permitting, follow an interesting and enjoyable route down the path to Ansteys Cove, around Redgate Beach and then rejoin the official path at Walls Hill. If you are taking the official route follow the road but shortly watch for a right turn through the woods signposted 'To Babbacombe & St. Marychurch over the Downs' which takes you to Walls Hill.

From Walls Hill the path will take you to the road descending to Babbacombe Beach, at the far end of which traverse a wooden bridge structure to Oddicombe beach where the path bears upwards just before the lower station of the Babbacombe Cliff Railway. You shortly pass under the railway and then take care to turn right downwards at the start of a pleasant path leading to a grassy picnic area where bear left uphill to join the track to Watcombe.

At the valley road linking the main Teignmouth/Torquay Road to Watcombe Beach turn left and immediately right, signpost Maidencombe 3/4 and follow a pleasant wooded path until you reach a path junction, where we think the present signposting is misleading. The inland path to the left is signed Coast Path Maidencombe with an 'acorn' and the new coastal path to the right is signed Maidencombe Alternative Route. There is also a small post with an 'acorn' and a yellow arrow pointing right. We hope this signposting will be changed, but do make sure you take the new path to the right which will bring you to the car park in Maidencombe. From the car park go a few yards up the road and turn right, unless you wish to visit the seasonal cafe a little further up the road.

From here there are some quite stiff gradients until you reach the road at Labrador where turn right and in a few yards leave the pavement to take a sunken path on your right and shortly enter a field on your right via a stile by a field gate.

Superb views now as you descend along the coastal side of the field system, then taking the path round The Ness to Shaldon.

NTG – Page 139. Paragraph 3 states 'after railway up and down'. In fact it is 'down and up'.

NTG – Page 141. The route shown between Valley of Rocks and Bell Rock is incorrect.

66 Shaldon to Exmouth via Topsham Ferry

OS 192 (V) Shaldon (T) Teignmouth (B.Rail) (T) Dawlish (B.Rail) (V) Dawlish Warren (B.Rail)
(V) Starcross (B.Rail)

Grading: Easy	Distance-	30	820	19	512

See also our Shaldon to Sidmouth Path Description

Distance is measured by diverting inland from the centre of Dawlish along the main road to Holcombe, and also includes the diversion inland to use the ferry at Topsham.

This is a section where you may have problems depending on the time of year and state of the tide.

Shaldon/Teignmouth (River Teign)
Teignbridge District Council, Resort Managers Office, Forde House, Newton Abbot, TQ12 4XX. Tel: Teignmouth (01626) 779770 Resort Manager or (01626) 779769 Tourist Information Centre.

All year round. 20 minutes service. May to October 7 days a week 0800–dusk. November to April Monday to Friday only 0800–1700.

After crossing from Shaldon by ferry follow the promenade past the pier and shortly you reach Eastcliff Walk forking up on your left and here you must make your first decision. The true route is ahead along the sea wall but at certain states of the high tide and particularly in bad weather it may be impossible after a two mile walk to pass under the railway line at the end of the wall, and if this appears likely a detour is needed. You should ascend Eastcliff Walk which soon becomes a track and will eventually lead you to the A379 where turn right and rejoin the coast path at the top of Smugglers Lane.

If conditions look right enjoy the walk along the sea wall and at the end pass under the railway line and ascend Smugglers Lane to the A379. Now you have a short walk on this busy main road, although there is a footpath on the left hand side, and after about 150 yards turn right into Derncleugh Gardens, then left into Windward Lane and take the path over a stile on your left. After a field section you are back on the road but immediately follow the Old Teignmouth Road on your right until you reach the main road yet again, turn right and shortly by some railings turn right and follow the path which soon zig-zags down to the boat cove and follow the sea wall to Dawlish Station.

From here it is possible at low tide to walk along the sea wall to Dawlish Warren, then at the start of the new promenade cross the railway by a footbridge to join the inland path and reach the main road. if the tide is high you must take the alternative route up the Exeter Road out of Dawlish and shortly after passing the new Rockstone Flats turn right on the road signposted Dawlish Warren 3/4 mile and immediately take the coastal footpath signed on your right to follow the Ladies Mile to Dawlish Warren. (You can in fact take a footpath immediately before the Rockstone Flats, although this is not signposted, then take the left fork to join the coastal path.)

There is no official path along the Warren but if time and energy permit you can enjoy a circular walk round this sandy Nature Reserve.

You are now faced with crossing the River Exe and in the summer months there is a ferry from Starcross to Exmouth reached by walking along the road from Dawlish Warren. However this is a busy road and you can if you wish catch one of the frequent buses to Starcross.

Starcross/Exmouth (River Exe)
Mr B Rackley,
Starcross Pier & Pleasure Company,
26 Marine Parade,
Dawlish.
Tel: (01626) 862452

From Starcross Pier.
Seasonal. 7 days a week.
1 May–mid October. 1000 hrs then every hour on the hour, last ferry 1745 hrs.
From Exmouth, Ferry Steps.
1030 hrs, then every hour on the half hour, last ferry 1815 hrs. Crossing approx. 15 minutes.

In winter and at other times when the ferry is not running, it is possible to catch a train from Dawlish Warren, changing at Exeter and going to Exmouth or to catch a bus at Exeter and cross over at Countess Wear and catch a bus to Exmouth.

When the Starcross/Exmouth ferry is not running you have the following alternatives.

1. You can catch a train at Dawlish Warren changing at Exeter and going back down to Exmouth.

2. You can do the same thing using the frequent bus services, changing over routes at either Countess Wear or in Exeter.

3. You can use the all year round ferry at Topsham to cross the River Exe. From Starcross continue by road to Powderham Church where a footpath follows the river and then the canal to a bridge across the canal where the ferry then crosses the river. (Care – this ferry is dependent on tide and weather, does not operate at lunchtime or on a Tuesday).

4. A new venture is Exe Water Taxis which will pick up passengers from the tip of Dawlish Warren and take them to Exmouth – contact Bob or Jenny Killick, 60 High Street Topsham EX3 0DY (01392 873409).

Topsham Ferry (River Exe)
Exeter City Council Canals & Rivers Dept.
Tel: 01392 74306.

All year round 6 days a week.
Oct./April 0800 1730 hrs. (Not Weekdays
Provisional – in any case Telephone 01392 74306)
May/Sept. 0800 2000 hrs.
Intervals between runs on request.
Closed all day Tuesday.
Dependent on tide and weather.

Once across the river you have to get to Exmouth and we are inclined to suggest the frequent bus service but failing this the walk as far as Lympstone will be on the road except for a small footpath section between Clyst Bridge and Ebford. From Lympstone there is a riverside path to Exmouth, now part of the East Devon Way – look for the mauve markers featuring a foxglove.

BMG – Page 29. The official path goes up and onto the point west of Shaldon – see NTG.

BMG – Page 31. When Starcross Ferry not running you need not go into Exeter – use Topsham Ferry – as above.

67	**Exmouth to Budleigh Salterton**		**OS 192 (T) Exmouth (B.Rail)**			

Grading: Moderate

	Distance-	10	830	6	518

See also our Shaldon to Sidmouth Path Description

No real problems here for walkers but keep inland of the range at Straight Point.

68	**Budleigh Salterton to Sidmouth**		**OS 192 (T) Budleigh Salterton**			

Grading: Starts moderate but becomes strenuous

	Distance-	11	841	7	525

See also our Shaldon to Sidmouth Path Description

The start is along a raised path inland to the River Otter Bridge at South Farm, then a riverside path back to the coast.

The path around High Peak is well marked but it does not unfortunately go over the top as you, and many others in the past, obviously expected. If you do battle your way to the top you will certainly not be disappointed with the views. The path on the top of Peak Hill immediately west of Sidmouth has been improved to give better seaward views.

The descent from Peak Hill towards Sidmouth takes you down through a wood and out on to the road. Cross the road into a field where a newly created path will separate you from busy traffic. You leave the field to cross the road again to parkland for the descent into Sidmouth. Later, flower lovers will prefer the longer route through the Connaught Gardens, but you have to come back to the road in the end.

69	Sidmouth to Seaton	OS 192 (T) Sidmouth

Grading: Strenuous	Distance-	15	856	9	534

See also our Sidmouth to Lyme Regis Path Description

Please note that there are a number of quite considerable ascents and descents on this section. Do not judge the effort required purely on the mileage. There are one or two places in this stretch where it is easy to come off the route but one is not likely to come to any severe harm.

After Branscombe Mouth there are alternative paths. The one over Hooken Cliffs gives superb views and is probably easier to walk. The undercliff path, apart from the beginning among the caravans is scenically better and we would recommend this if the weather is good. You have the interesting undercliff itself, the massive cliffs to the left, interesting rock formations ahead, and good views to seaward. At most states of the tide it is possible to walk along the beach from Seaton Hole to Seaton, avoiding some road work.

WATCH THE TIDE – YOU CAN GET CUT OFF.

CP – The path is nearer the coast than the map suggests between Weston Cliff and Branscombe Mouth.

NTG – From Branscombe Mouth to Beer Head the map does not show the path along the top of Hooken Cliffs only through Under Hooken. It is mentioned in the text. Both routes are official.

NTG – Between Coxe's Cliff and Branscombe the old route is described. Map is also wrong.

BMG – The old route is shown east of Littlecombe Shoot.

70	Seaton to Lyme Regis	OS 193 (T) Seaton

Grading: Moderate	Distance-	12	868	8	542

See also our Sidmouth to Lyme Regis Path Description

You leave Seaton across its concrete bridge over the River Axe and have to turn inland. Then, go up the road to the golf course then walk due East across the fairway into a lane, along it and in less than 1/4 mile turn right to the coast.

The section through the Landslip is in a National Nature Reserve and can be very rewarding to some but extremely frustrating to others. Views are extremely limited and the path in places puts on a fair imitation of a corkscrew or helter-skelter; you are unlikely to get lost but most unlikely to know where you are. Suggested times to walk the Landslip range from 1½ hours to 4 hours, but we are told that the standard time is about 3 hours.

The path into Lyme Regis has now been improved and you can take a path directly down to The Cobb without having to come into the car park and then down the road.

BMG – Page 70. The path does not enter a car park above Lyme Regis. It is through fields direct to The Cobb.

Grading: Moderate   Distance-   4   872   2   544

This is a difficult section owing to the very insecure nature of the cliffs. Dorset County Council have worked to provide a series of routes here but they are up against a continual problem of slipping cliffs. There have had to be necessary diversions. The last incidence of erosion has prompted the Golf Club to ban all coast path walkers from the edge of their course. This has resulted in Dorset County Council diverting the path to well inland around most of the golf course, and here we are, eight years later, still awaiting Coast Path reinstatement. We think we ought to tell you that having entered Dorset now that it is the slowest at making good any gaps caused by landslides and also that it has a piece of so-called Coastal Path furthest away from the coast. Having said that, it does have many sections of extremely good walking if only the county would establish a true coast path which is, after all, what it is supposed to be.

At the time of going to print we have been advised that agreement has been reached between the golf club and Dorset County Council over a strip of land for a new Coast Path. However for this edition we still include details of the official diversion with our own modifications. If you are lucky enough to find the new path in place 'on the ground' when you come to this section it should be signposted. In any case it is not difficult to follow as it is routed between the golf course and the cliff edge.

From Lyme Regis town centre take Church Street and Charmouth Road (A3052) until you reach Lyme Regis Football Club on the right, beyond which you will find a stile at the corner of a lane and take the footpath across fields to a lane where you turn left (yes west!) for 50 yds. At a finger post sign turn right up through the wood and near the top you will find another such sign, this time with a notice and map about the diversion. Turn left and follow a narrow path to join a minor road, and turn right up the hill past the Golf Club to rejoin the main A3052 road. In about 100 yards on the right, at the sign post to Fern Hill, take the footpath running east. You will drop down across fairways (take care!) into woodlands and follow the path which curves to the north to regain the A3052 road again, and turn right. Beyond the junction of this road with the new A35 Charmouth Bypass, watch out for steps on the right to a stile and public footpath. This will take you through Lily Farm and across a field where you come to a lane. Turn right and within 50 yards left and carry forward on to the coast.

We recommend a low tide diversion along the beach between Lyme Regis and Charmouth especially if the tide is well out because the sand is very firm here. On no account should attempts be made to walk upon the surface of the huge grey mud slide. When the tide permits, keep to seaward on firm sand.

CP – See paragraph above for route through Lily Farm. It is not as that shown on map.

NTG – There is no route alongside the golf course on Timber Hill as shown on the map, although it is referred to in the text. We think this important because many walkers try to work from maps first. This map does show you our recommended track through Lily Farm rather than Dorset County Council's advised route along the main road.

72 | **Charmouth to West Bay**   **OS 193 1 mile to (V) Charmouth**

Grading: Strenuous   Distance-   11   883   7   551

Interesting walking with spectacular views from Golden Cap, the highest mainland point on the south coast of England and later from Thorncombe Beacon. However, be warned, your good views are not obtained without effort!

When you get to what looks like the top of Golden Cap you have to turn left and go a little higher to the trig. point to find your way down, which starts at the north end before later swinging east again.

Grading: Moderate Distance- 15 898 9 560

SEE SECTION 79 FOR DETAILS OF THE ALTERNATIVE INLAND COAST PATH FROM WEST BEXINGTON TO OSMINGTON MILLS.

Leaving West Bay do not go seaward again immediately after you have walked round the back of the harbour. Pass to the right of St. John's Church and carry forward to the West Bay Hotel ahead, opposite which is the Coast Path sign pointing at an angle across a gravel area to the foot of surprisingly steep cliffs. If you go seaward in West Bay too soon you will give yourself a hard stretch along coarse shingle.

Watch for the inland diversion at Burton Freshwater. When the river is low you can 'cut the corner' across the beach but this is not at all possible when the river is flowing strongly; do not try it, you will surely drown! As you start to descend to the caravan park you can look across and see if the river is not reaching the sea, then it is up to you.

At Burton Bradstock Beach just after the hotel the old seasonal cafe that burnt down has been rebuilt by the National Trust, and is leased out by them.

At Burton Mere, unless you are particularly interested in maritime flowers, it is nearly always better to go inland of the Mere, rather than go along the seaward side. You will get quite enough pebbles later.

There is a seasonal cafe at West Bexington, and seasonal snack wagons in the 'car park where the road turns inland past Abbotsbury Gardens. Walkers, however, should continue along for another couple of hundred yards.

Refreshments, shops and B & B's in Abbotsbury. If you have time the climb up to St Catherine's Chapel is worth the effort.

A permissive path runs to the Swannery from the coast path that contours to the seaward side of Chapel Hill.

Grading: Easy – Chesil Beach: Strenuous Distance- 23 921 14 574

See also our Abbotsbury to Weymouth path Description

SEE SECTION 80 FOR DETAILS OF THE OPTIONAL EXTRA ROUTE AROUND THE ISLE OF PORTLAND.

Presumably you must have wanted to go into Abbotsbury if you did visit the village, but it is worth mentioning that the path does not really go there at all, but only close to it. Therefore, the correct, and sometimes quieter, way out is by the footpath going south to Nunnery Grove, and not the road by Mill Farm.

The path unfortunately now goes over a mile inland, despite our efforts. The inland path is well marked and enjoyable to walk, part of it along a ridge and with some good views. You do not get back to the shores of the Fleet until Rodden Hive.

On the outskirts of Abbotsbury after Horsepool Farm keep going up the ridge, beguiling, much better tracks go round the hill to the right, but they will not bring you to the stile you need at the top. In about 1 mile turn south off to the ridge and turn sharp left after Hodder's Coppice. A track goes forward, but this is NOT the one you want. After you have crossed a minor road, the official path follows the field headland east and then south to the north east corner of Wyke Wood as signposted, and not in a direct line as shown on some maps. Take particular care as you approach Rodden Hive – the path suddenly dives through a hedge on your left. There is an apparent track and even a marker post which might make you think that the path goes to the right of the stream, but it does not.

At Tidmoor Point, one may have to divert if firing on the range is in progress across the definitive right of way. A diversion has been made inland at Wyke Regis for a Service Establishment.

At Ferry Bridge you have the opportunity to extend your walk by including a coastal circuit of the Isle of Portland. The route is outlined in Section 80.

A footpath sign has now been erected to show you where to continue on to Weymouth, but not where to leave the old railway line (at the north end of the shallow cutting) to get back to the coast path. Signs are very sparse in Weymouth to encourage you – we have asked for improvements. Pass the sailing centre and continue into Old Castle Road; opposite Castle Cove Sailing Club bear right onto a tarmac footpath. Continue on paths close to the coast to Nothe Fort and bear sharp left down to the harbourside which is followed to the Town Bridge, which is crossed and the opposite side of the harbour is followed back to the Pavilion Complex. Here bear left to join The Esplanade. In summer a little ferry may run across the harbour to shorten the route.

An alternative for the tough walker who wishes to stay on the coast is to use the Chesil Beach; this is, of course, much more attractive since the inland route has been worsened. You can do this by going onto the beach where the path turns inland at Abbotsbury but note you cannot 'get off' again until you reach the causeway from Wyke Regis to Portland. This is only a walk for the fit and not one to be attempted at times of severe gale! Please note that the Chesil Bank is closed to visitors from 1st May–31st August for the Schedule 1 bird nesting season. During the nesting season please keep to the seaward side of the beach so as not to interfere with nesting birds.

Weymouth Harbour
Weymouth & Portland Borough Council,
Harbour Master's Office,
Municipal Offices, PO Box 21,
North Quay, Weymouth, DT4 8TA
(01305-206363) Ask for Dep. Borough Engineer.

Seasonal. Easter–October Daily.
Continuous if passengers are waiting
and weather permits.

NTG – The definitive path is now around the edge of Langton Hive Point. It no longer makes the loop inland as shown. North of Wyke Wood the path is as described above.

| 75 | Weymouth to Lulworth Cove | OS 194 (T) Weymouth (B.Rail) |

Grading: This section runs the gamut from easy to moderate to strenuous. Distance- 19   940   12   586

See also our Weymouth to Lulworth Cove Path Description

SEE SECTION 79 FOR DETAILS OF THE ALTERNATIVE INLAND COAST PATH FROM WEST BEXINGTON TO OSMINGTON MILLS.

The start along the seafront at Weymouth has been called uninteresting but at least you are in sight of the sea all the way. When the promenade comes to an end opt for walking along the wall behind the beach; this keeps you away from the traffic and gives you the best view, as long as you do not fall off! At Overcombe where the path leaves the road there is no proper route signposted at the time of writing; the official route should go up the minor road to Bowleaze Cove. However, after passing the Spyglass Inn it is best to cross the grass public open space and follow the cliff edge to the Beachside Centre. After Pontin's Riviera Holiday Centre the cliff is sliding away and the path with it. However, a slight diversion on stable ground is possible.

At the stile at the eastern end of the Pontin's Holiday Camp, this is the second Pontin's establishment and is shown as Short Lake House on maps, it is important that you follow the sign. It does in fact point in the right direction; compass carriers check it – it's about 72°. You go up over the hill apparently going inland – you do not follow the cliff edge.

On the downhill approach to Osmington Mills the new route avoiding the landslide bears away from the cliff edge over a stile and down the right hand side of a field. At the bottom it joins the Alternative Inland Route just before it crosses two stiles to meet the narrow road that is followed down to the coast. The new route is signposted.

At Ringstead one is taken inland, although the official path should go along the seafront. At the old coastguard cottages at White Nothe, be careful to take the left fork of the two yellow arrows, that being the correct route. From White Nothe onwards you will find that there are some quite severe gradients to be traversed before you reach Lulworth.

There is an unfortunate diversion slightly inland on the last stretch down to Lulworth Cove, however, some people turn even further inland than they need. Some new signposts have been erected in the Lulworth Cove area indicating 'Youth Hostel–Coast Path' and contain the acorn emblem. These signs are intended to indicate the route to the Youth Hostel at East Lulworth and are not the continuation of the Coast Path.

The nimble who wish to arrive at Lulworth by a quieter, non-car-park route, should, on Hambury Tout, turn right and take the old track down on the right-hand side of the fence. This links with the beach path to St Oswald's Bay. On reaching this turn left. Presently, it comes to a tarmac road which you can follow into Lulworth.

NTG – The route shown in the map from Hambury Tout to West Lulworth is the alternative and not the true Coast Path which keeps to seaward and is much more pleasant than walking through a huge car park.

| 76 | Lulworth Cove to Kimmeridge, Gaulter Gap | | OS 194 and 195 (V) Lulworth |

| Grading: Severe | Distance- | 11 | 951 | 7 | 593 |

See also our Lulworth to Kimmeridge Path Description

The coastal path through the Army Ranges is now open again at certain times, see below. It is a very fine walk indeed but a tough one. If closed, we now include the walk around, see below.

At most states of the tide, it is perfectly possible to walk along the pebble beach at Lulworth Cove, going up the path which rises diagonally on the far side of the beach. At the top of the steep ascent off the beach, the best route proceeds seawards and there the path turns eastwards along the coast to the beginning of the Army Ranges, just by the Fossil Forest.

If, unfortunately, time should be of the essence, when you have crossed the beach and gone up the path, do not turn right but go straight ahead. This way you will come to the Bindon Gate into the range, and you can go ahead here coming out on the coast again at Mupe Bay. It is a little shorter but far less scenic. At Gaulter Gap keep to the seaward side of the cottage unless you want the toilets which are situated beyond the north end.

RAC Gunnery School Lulworth Ranges: No Firing and Firing Periods

1. *NON FIRING PERIOD*. The Range Walks will be open to the public during the following holiday periods, all dates are inclusive.:

EASTER 1995	14 APR 95–23 APR 95
SPRING 1995	27 MAY 95–04 JUN 95
SUMMER 1995	29 JUL 95–03 SEP 95
CHRISTMAS/NEW YEAR 1995/96	22 DEC 95–O2 JAN 96

2. *FIRING PERIODS*. The Range Walks are normally open to the public every Saturday and Sunday except for some weekends in the year. For 1995 they have reserved the following 6 weekends for firing:

FIRST WEEKEND	18–19 FEB 95
SECOND	18–19 MAR 95
THIRD	06–07 MAY 95
FOURTH	17–18 JUN 95
FIFTH	07–08 OCT 95
SIXTH	11–12 NOV 95

3. Experience has shown that it is sometimes possible to avoid firing on some of these reserved weekends and if this is the case the Range Walks will be opened. Should this occur in 1995 we will make every effort to publicise the fact.

4. Tyneham Church and the School are normally open for viewing 0900 hrs–1500 hrs when the walks are open.

5. Information is also available from:

    a. The Range Control Office (0900–1630 hrs Mon–Fri and during the six weekend firing periods). Telephone: Bindon Abbey 01929-462721 Ext 4819/4859.

    b. The Guardroom (at any time). Telephone: Bindon Abbey 01929 462721 Ext 4824.

Unfortunately, there are no permanent staff on duty in the Guardroom. Soldiers posted to or on a course at Lulworth find themselves on Guard Duty from time to time. They have much to do and whether or not the Range Walks are open does not come to the top of the list. Every effort is made to ensure that up to date information is at hand at the Guardroom.

Alternative Route when Lulworth Range Coast Path is unavailable: Lulworth Cove to Kimmeridge, Gaulter Gap

Option 1 – 13¹/₂ miles on safer, quieter but more strenuous route using mainly rights of way, and permissive paths through Lulworth Park (pre-plotting of given grid refs. onto map will assist navigation).

Leave the Cove and take 2nd road left (825807). 100 yds on right, a footpath leads north for ³/₄ mile; turn right (east) and after 100 yds left (north) to pass Belhuish Coppice and Belhuish Carm, and then across B3071 at 835832.

At 844(5)828 eastern boundary of Burngate Wood, use permissive (blue) path north-east past Park Lodge, and across road (855832) onto bridleway.

(The permissive red path across the stile, just up on the left, loops around the lake – if you're ready for a peaceful stop – and meets this bridleway further up at 861[5]834.)

Continue NE along bridleway to 865839 where it veers north, and later north-east through Highwood to meet road at 872862. Road walk east, fork right (signposted Stoborough) at 88258555; over crossroads at 886855 east for further 1¹/₂ miles along Holme Lane to 912855.

(*) Turn right just before a hump-back railway bridge onto Dorey Farm bridleway at 912855. After 1¹/₄ miles turn right onto Creech Road leading south-southwest towards the Purbeck Ridge. Another 1¹/₂ miles road walk up a steep gradient to a viewpoint car park. Beyond the car park 902815 take the left road that turns back and down over the ridge to Corfe. (A short cut bridleway 905817 zig-zags down to meet the same road.) As the road levels out at a left hand bend 907812, take the bridleway ahead that leads out south through Steeple Leaze Farm.

200 yds south of the farm a footpath leads south crossing another ridge bridleway, down a steep path, and across a field to Higher Stonehips, and on to Gaulter Gap, the easterly point of the range walks.

Option 2 – 12 miles of mainly road walking. Care needed on narrow bends.

Leave the Cove to West Lulworth on the B3071, and then turn right to East Lulworth on the B3070. After 3 miles turn right (east) at 886855 along Holme Lane, and then continue from (*) above, at 912855.

77	Kimmeridge, Gaulter Gap to Swanage			OS 195

Grading: Severe and then moderate	Distance-	19	970	12	605

See also our Kimmeridge to South Haven Point Path Description

From Gaulter Gap, Kimmeridge, there is a good path all the way to Chapman's Pool. There have been landslides between Chapman's Pool and St Albans Head in the undercliff area. Unfortunately, we have had to agree to a new high level route, and this has increased the distance by about one mile. The path is very well signposted in general. There is one place, after you have turned inland where you reach a gate in a field by a cattle grid, where you could go wrong. You must not go over the cattle grid where the signpost says, 'The Beach is Closed' but instead follow the path which bears inland up the valley and when the houses are reached there are plenty of signs to guide you from there on.

The first part of the climb up West Hill is uninteresting and sadly away from shoulder and views. However as you gain height going along Emmets Hill views back along the Dorset Coast are very good indeed. Do not miss the new Royal Marines memorial just to the left of the path and be sure to read the inscription.

From St Albans Head there is fine high level waking all the way to Durlston Head. There is not much accommodation along this stretch. There is a poor bus service from Worth Matravers to Swanage, so plan ahead.

There is a total absence of signing in the Durlston Country Park. Again we have asked for improvement so it may be there when you get there. However, you keep on the low level path all the way around Durlston Head but as you come up on the north side of it you take the second turning right not the first which is a dead end into a quarry.

The section of the coastal path is not very clear in and around Swanage, but you are unlikely to get badly lost.

CP – The map suggests that the Coast Path enters Worth Matravers. It does not. It turns sharply south through the word 'Farm' of Renscombe Farm.

---

78 | Swanage to Sandbanks (South Haven Point) OS 195 (T) Swanage. (V) Studland

Grading: Moderate Distance- 12 982 8 613

See also our Kimmeridge to South Haven Point Path Description

At Ocean Bay Stores at the north end of Swanage Sea Front, tide permitting, it was usually better to keep along the pedestrian promenade to the end and then walk 200 yards along the beach turning up some steps rather than take the poor Official route. Because of another landslip this route cannot be used now and you have to follow the latter route leave the seafront on the main road (Ulwell Road) and where it bears left into a one-way system continue ahead into Redcliffe Road. At the sub Post Office turn sharp right into Ballard Way and at the end do not be put off by the signs 'Ballard Private Estate'. Carry forward into the quaint little estate of chalets and follow signs for the Coast Path to emerge on to a grassed area on the cliff edge.

Signposting is bad in Studland. As you come in you reach a road junction by a public toilet. Here turn right. You will then pass two Public Footpath signs pointing right, but do not take either of them. Eventually, you will come to The Manor House Hotel. It is the track/road down to the beach after this hotel that you require. When you get down to the beach, turn left. When the tide is out this is firm, but when it is in more effort is required. Maybe too we should warn those who do not know, that this is a naturist beach, so you must not be put off if you find on this last lap that you are the only one wearing clothes!

Wainwright at the end of his work on the Pennine Way said it all, and said it better, of a shorter path. Ward & Mason in the old Letts Guide simply say 'That's it'. We will add whether you have been lucky enough to walk the whole way from Minehead at one go, or simply, as most of us have, in bits and pieces over a period, nonetheless you will be glad you walked and have just finished Britain's longest and finest footpath. It's a longer step than most take in their lifetime!

IF YOU WISH TO WALK ON, THE BOURNEMOUTH COAST PATH LINKS THE END OF THE SOUTH WEST WAY WITH THE RECENTLY WAYMARKED SOLENT WAY, GIVING A CONTINUOUS PATH FROM MINEHEAD TO EMSWORTH

Studland/Sandbanks (Mouth of Poole Harbour) Bournemeouth-Swanage Motor Road & Ferry Company, Shell Bay, Studland. BH19 3BA.
Tel: Studland (01929) 44203.

All year round. Every 20 minutes, less during peak periods. Late ferry 2300 hrs. At weekends and throughout the summer every night.

Grading: Moderate   Distance-   **29**   **18**

Although this is certainly not a coastal path it is an enjoyable walk along a well-marked path with good views seaward from the ridges. Because it is inland a more detailed route is given. When walking this section bear in mind that we found no place for obtaining refreshments between the start of the walk, where there is a cafe, and the village of Osmington.

At West Bexington car park turn inland up the road signposted 'Inland Route – Coast Path', and where the road turns left, continue forward up a stony track, signposted 'Hardy Monument 5¹/₂ miles'. At top of the hill the footpath briefly joins the main road but you immediately leave again over the stile on the right through the field, signposted 'Hardy Monument 5 miles'. Take care, the way across this field is not clear and one must keep to the bottom end of the field and not stay along the top wire fence. After you have crossed wall, you can start to bear upwards to the left to the further signpost near the road, marked with the acorn symbol and the words 'Inland Route'. After about 300 yards continuing through the field and by the corner of a wall there is a further signpost 'Hardy Monument 4¹/₂, Osmington Mills 15'. Continue forward, very shortly emerging on to the B3157 road which you cross and leave through a gate, signposted 'Hardy Monument 4¹/₂'.

You now approach Abbotsbury Castle and where the path in front divides take the right-hand fork along the front of the Fort past the trig point, from where you can get superb views in all directions, and you should be able to see clearly Hardy's Monument in the distance showing you the way forward. Proceed forward and cross the minor road now and go forward, signpost 'Hardy Monument 4'. Proceed in an approximate easterly direction along the ridge of Wears Hill and the crest of White Hill for about two miles following the signposts and waymarks. However be careful not to follow signs with the acorn symbol incorrectly shown that indicate routes down to the village of Abbotsbury lying in the valley below, with the old chapel clearly visible. At the east end of White Hill bear north east as signposted and leave in the inland corner through a gate on to a minor road. Turn left along the road for approximately 30 yards and then turn right, signposted 'Inland Route – Hardy Monument 2'. Follow the bridleway marked with blue arrows along the wire fence above the scrub to a stile where the blue bridleway arrow points to the right and the yellow footpath arrow with acorn indicates the way forward. At the far side of the field the track then leads approximately 50 yards to a further gate with stile and waymark. Immediately adjacent to this gate is a stone circle which is an ancient monument and there is a sign to this effect. One now continues forward, leaving a small wood to the left, to reach the road from Portisham to Winterbourne Steepleton. Turn left along the road for approximately 40 yards and then turn right into a field over a stile, signposted 'Hardy Monument 1¹/₂ – Osmington Mills 13'. On the far side of the field proceed forward, signpost 'Hardy Monument 1'. At this point there is a signpost forking right to Hellstone only with a return possible on a different path.

At Blackdown Barn turn left to climb up through the woods, signpost 'Hardy Monument ¹/₂'. At the monument you will find a small signpost 'Inland Route – Osmington Mills 11 miles' with a blue arrow indicating the way forward. Cross the road to a further signpost with acorn symbol and now descend through the bracken. One shortly reaches the road again, turn left and in a few yards ignore the signpost on the right, cutting back indicating 'Bridleway to Coast Path' and continue forward, signpost 'Coast Path East' and in another 50 yards turn right, signpost 'Inland Route to Courton Hill' on one side of the sign and 'Osmington 12 – Courton Hill 2' on the other. Now there is a good ridgeway path without navigational problems for some 8 miles and good views to the seaward in the distance. After passing the radio mast you come to the B3159 marked by the Borough of Weymouth boundary stone, continue across the road, signposted 'Inland Route East'.

On reaching the A354 turn right immediately before the main road down the signposted track and after just over ¹/₄ mile you will find a stile in the hedge on your left. The path leads across a narrow field to cross the busy A354. Before the farm with its adjacent radio mast take care to go through the gate on the right, marked with a blue arrow, but this time also with the acorn symbol. After crossing the field, leaving two tumuli to your left, you reach a metalled road. Turn right and at the next junction there is a signpost surmounted by a symbol 'Dorset – Came Wood' which, unusually, carries the six-figure map reference of the locality. Here you turn right at the signpost 'Bridleway to Bincombe' and the acorn symbol. At the end of the path join a metalled road and at the junction turn left, signposted 'Inland Route East'.

Drop down the road into the village of Bincombe and where the road turns right take the track up leaving a small church on your right. Where the path splits take the left-hand fork signposted again with a blue arrow and the acorn symbol. After the overhead high-voltage power lines pass through a small signposted wooden gate and then proceed forward through one field into the next to the footpath sign. Here turn half left, following the line of the old indistinct curving grassy track until it meets the road at the bottom of Combe Valley. Turn left here and follow the road until you reach the Combe Valley road sign to 'Sutton Poyntz' and take this turn to the right. After 50 yards turn left through a gate, signposted 'White Horse Hill – Osmington Mills'. The path now is easy to follow with extensive views to seaward over Weymouth and Portland. On passing a ruined building on your left you reach a broad track and turn right, signposted 'Osmington 1½' and after about 300 yards leave the track through a gate on the right, signposted 'Inland Route Osmington'. You will shortly pass the trig point on your right and at the next field gate turn left and follow the field boundary along White Horse Hill. Just beyond the next gate fork right, signpost 'Osmington 1, Lulworth 8'.

Descend to the village of Osmington and follow the signs through the village. When you reach the main Weymouth road at the Sun Ray Inn turn left and in about 250 yards turn right at a signpost, over a stile and footbridge, and follow the field boundary on the left through two fields and at the top look back to see Hardy's Monument in the distance and also the white horse on the hillside. Go over the stile to the footpath sign, turn half right to cross the field at an angle to a further stile. Cross it and turn left along the hedge side to the bottom. At the end of the field there is a very short length of enclosed footpath to the road, turn right along it descending to Osmington Mills.

---

80 | Optional extra route around the Isle of Portland   OS 194

Grading: Moderate   **Distance (from Ferry Bridge) –   22   14**

If you have time to spare a circuit of the Isle of Portland, although at present not part of the definitive route of the South West Coast Path, is well worth the extra effort. While it lacks the beauty of other parts of the coast path in Dorset, it is still a fine walk with much of interest as well as the rugged grandeur of the coast, which can be very spectacular in rough weather. To use its full name, The Island and Royal Manor of Portland, the 'island' is heavily occupied (at present) by the Ministry of Defence, and HM Prison Services, and shows many scars of extensive quarrying for its famous limestone.

From Ferry Bridge you have a number of choices, none of them of much merit, for the first two miles: Using the footway beside the busy A354 road; crossing over the car park beyond the Chesil Beach Centre to slog along the pebbles of Chesil Beach, or catching a bus to the roundabout at the south end of the causeway to alight at the Royal Victoria Lodge. This is Fortuneswell where you need to cross the road and follow signs for the Chesil Beach Gallery, turning left before the public toilets. Continue past the Cove House Inn and bear right up onto the promenade. Towards the end of this and just before the 'grassy walls', bear left and immediately left again up a zig zag path; then right past the school and up the steep path in the grass incline to the final steps to the road.

Briefly rejoin the main road (A354 – New Road) and bear off right at the hairpin bend onto the coast path running between old quarry banks and the shear cliff face. Three miles of spectacular and airy cliff top walking brings you to Portland Bill with the Pulpit Rock and lighthouse. Continue around the end of the low headland and pass to the seaward of wooden chalets to follow a winding path along the top of low cliffs to join a road above Freshwater Bay after about 1½ miles.

Turn right up the road for 600 yards, past Cheyne Weares Car Park to a finger post on the right. Follow the zig zag path down into the rugged undercliff area, and follow the waymarks through the disused quarry workings down to Church Ope Cove.

Before the 'West Cliff' and 'Coast Path' signs turn right through a gap in the hedge with 'Crown Estate' sign on to the undercliff path. Continue to seaward along the rugged path to Durdle Pier and bear up left to turn right onto a wide firm path (old track bed of the former Weymouth to Easton railway line). Continue along the track to just before a rifle range sign where it is necessary to turn left over a bank to follow a rocky path that climbs up the cliffs to an isolated chimney seen above on the skyline. A word of warning here – although the track continues northwards and appears to be well used do not be tempted to continue as the way forward is eventually blocked by the perimeter security fence of the MOD Establishments and there is no other route up the high cliffs.

At the chimney turn sharp right along a prison road, and follow a tarmac road northwards through a gap in a high wall. At the next road turn right and bear down hill toward the gates of the MOD establishment, but shortly go left at a fork through a barrier gate. Continue forward to a left hand bend, and carry on ahead on a grassy path towards a large pinnacle of rock after which, at the 'rock falls' sign, bear left steeply up on to the higher escarpment heading for a large communications mast. At the high wire perimeter fence turn left and follow the fence along and then around to the north to the entrance of Verne Prison. Take a path through a little gap to the left of the entrance, passing beside railings and down steep steps. Bear right along a path that traverses under the grassy banks and emerge onto a hairpin bend.

Turn left and past house number 90 to take a footpath down left. Emerging onto a road bear left, and take path beside a 'No Entry' sign to Ventnor Road. Walk down to Fortuneswell Road, and cross road to a path through a play park and turn right onto the road to the roundabout by the Royal Victoria Lodge. From here retrace your steps for the two miles to Ferry Bridge.

CALLIGRAPHIC MAP OF
THE SOUTH WEST WAY

This quality, partially coloured, printed calligraphic map
of the South West Way, was written entirely by hand and is
complemented by fine pen and ink drawings illustrating many of
the sights to be found whilst walking the path.
Overall size 560mm (22") deep by 760mm (30") wide. A print of
this calligraphic map, laminated (or unlaminated – suitable for
framing) costs £7.75 inclusive of postage and packing.
Orders, or requests for a leaflet describing the map in more detail
(SAE please) to: James Skinner (HB), 49 Appleton Way,
Hucclecote, Gloucester GL3 3RP.

**FOR EVERY PRINT ORDERED,
A SMALL DONATION WILL BE MADE TO THE SOUTH WEST
WAY ASSOCIATION'S FUNDS.**

ACCOMMODATION

This list of accommodation has been prepared in path order anti-clockwise.

Regarding the left-hand column

P = Packed lunches available.
O = Open all the year.
D = Drying facilities for wet clothes.

The part of the address in CAPITALS is an aid to location. It does not signify the postal town. The extreme right hand column refers to the appropriate section in the "Trail Description" part. We think it might help walkers find addresses quickly. The amount in brackets after the address gives an indication of the starting price for bed and breakfast. If working on a tight budget it is best to ask first.

In respect of the hostels listed, greater details will be found in the Hostel Handbook, available from Youth Hostels Association (England & Wales), St Albans, Herts. AL1 2DY. In particular watch the closed periods of the hostels.

The majority of our B & B address have been submitted by members. The fact that they are included in this book does not indicate a recommendation by The South West Way Association. Their inclusion is merely for information purposes, there they are, if you want them. We cannot, for financial and practical reasons, introduce vetting, inspection or any form of 'Star' rating. We do have a system whereby addresses can be removed from the list.

We wish to develop this list especially for many 'sparse' areas. Suggestions for inclusion in our next list will be welcome. Details of any new accommodation should be addressed to the Membership Secretary. Our list is not comprehensive, walkers will find many B&B's in towns and villages along the coast path that are not recorded in this book.

It would not be out of place here to add a word of thanks from those who walk to those who kindly board. How many times have we been thankful for a friendly welcome and good 'digs'? Maybe a note we had from one of our accommodation addresses puts it well. "We have had quite a lot of walkers this year and we have usually managed to dry them out – and feed them up."

Although there are a lot of addresses that state they are 'open all the year', some of these close for the Christmas period. Walkers should remember that during the holiday season many of our accommodation addresses could be fully booked up in advance by holidaymakers staying for a week or two. Conversely a walker could book up for one night only in good time thus preventing a guest house proprietor from taking a week or more booking later on. Accommodation problems can be frustrating to all parties concerned so bear these facts in mind when bed hunting.

During your initial contact with your selected host you could ask – 'Do you pick up and return to the coast path?' 'Do you provide early breakfasts?'And, if it should bother you that much, 'are there smokers in the house?'

TOURIST INFORMATION CENTRES can be a source of B & B addresses. If you have difficulties in booking accommodation then they should be approached. To help we have included details of TIC's in the appropriate path order in this accommodation section.

Important If having booked ahead, and for some reason or other you do not arrive at your accommodation address please telephone and explain your absence to your intended host. We have known instances where the host has become so worried about the non-appearance of walkers that they have informed the emergency services. The last thing we want is Police, Coastguards and Royal Navy helicopters out on a wild goose chase.

P	O	D	Name and Address	Telephone No.	Map Ref.	Section
			SOMERSET			
			YOUTH HOSTEL MINEHEAD – SEE Y.H.A. SECTION PAGE			
			Tourist Information Centre, 17 Friday Street, MINEHEAD, Somerset.	01643 702624		1
*	*	*	Mrs D Morris, Badgers, 38 Summerland Road, MINEHEAD, Somerset. (£12.50)	01643 704583		1
*	*	*	Mr M Morris, The Parks Hotel, The Parks, MINEHEAD, Somerset, TA24 8BT. (£15.00)	01643 703547	965 463	1
*	*	*	Mr S Phillips, The Old Ship Aground, Quay Street, MINEHEAD, Somerset, TA24 5UL. (£12.50)	01643 702078		1
	*		Mr & Mrs J & A Segenhout, Mayfair Hotel, The Avenue, MINEHEAD, Somerset, TA24 5AY. (£23.00)	01643 702719		1
*	*	*	Mr E Bower, Countrywide Holidays, Doverhay Place, PORLOCK, Somerset, TA24 8EX. (£17.00)	01643 862398	891 468	1
*	*	*	Mrs S Coombs, Hurlstone, Sparkhayes Lane, PORLOCK, Somerset. (£14.00)	01643 862650	887 469	1
*	*	*	Mr D Fewell, Orchard House, Bossington, PORLOCK, Somerset, TA24 8HQ. (£16.00)	01643 862336	897 479	1
*	*	*	Mrs E J Richards, Silcombe Farm, PORLOCK, Somerset, TA24 8JN. (£14.50)	01643 862248		1
*	*	*	Mr & Mrs M & J Robinson, The Ship Inn, High Street, PORLOCK, Somerset, TA24 8QD. (£16.50)	01643 862507		1
*	*	*	Mrs J Stiles-Cox, Leys, The Ridge, Off Bossington Lane, PORLOCK, Somerset, TA24 8HA. (£15.00)	01643 862477	892 469	1
	*	*	Mr D Thorne, Myrtle Cottage, High Street, PORLOCK, Somerset TA24 8PU. (£16.00)	01643 862978	885 468	1
*	*	*	Mr & Mrs R G Thornton, Lorna Doone Hotel, High Street, PORLOCK, Somerset, TA24 8PS. (£18.50)	01643 862404	888 468	1
*	*	*	Mrs B Starr, Sea View Cottage, PORLOCK WEIR, Somerset. (£14.00)	01643 862523	864 478	1
			NORTH DEVON			
			YOUTH HOSTELS LYNTON, ILFRACOMBE – SEE Y.H.A. SECTION PAGE			
*	*	*	Mr & Mrs C Clifford, Tregonwell, Riverside G.H., 1 Tors Road, LYNMOUTH, Devon, EX35 6ET. (£16.50)	01598 753369	726 494	2
*		*	North Cliff Hotel, North Walk, LYNMOUTH, Devon, EX35 6HJ. (£22.50)	01598 752357		2

P	O	D	Name and Address	Telephone No.	Map Ref.	Section
*	*	*	Mrs J Pile, Oakleigh, 4 Tors Road, LYNMOUTH, Devon, EX35 6ET. (£16.00)	01598 752220		2
*		*	Mr & Mrs Price, East Lyn House Hotel, Watersmeet Road, LYNMOUTH, Devon, EX35 6EP. (£22.00)	01598 752540		2
*	*	*	Mrs P E Morgan, Kingford House, Longmead, LYNTON, Devon. (£17.50)	01598 752361		2
*	*	*	Mr & Mrs J & R Oborne, The Retreat, No 1 Park Gardens, Lydiate Lane, LYNTON, Devon, EX35 6DF. (£15.00)	01598 753526		2
*	*	*	Woodlands Hotel, Lynbridge Road, LYNTON, Devon, EX35 6AX. (£18.00)	01598 752324	721 488	2
			Tourist Information Centre, Town Hall, Lee Road, LYNTON, Devon, EX35 6BT.	01598 752225		2
*		*	Mrs Dallyn, Mannacott Farm, Nr Hunters Inn, MARTINHOE, Devon. (£13.00)	01598 3227	663 482	2
*	*	*	Mr & Mrs F J Barry, Glendower, King Street, COMBE MARTIN, Devon, EX34 0AL (£12.00)	01271 883449		3
*		*	Mrs J Bosley, Hillview Guest House, The Woodlands, COMBE MARTIN, Devon. (£14.00)	01271 882331	575 469	3
*		*	Mr & Mrs Clarke, Wynnestead, King Street, COMBE MARTIN, Devon. (£11.50)	01271 883363		3
*	*	*	Mr R Leonard, The Fo'c's'le, Seaside, COMBE MARTIN, Devon, EX34 0DJ. (£15.00)	01271 883354		3
*	*	*	Mrs M Mangnall, Moorlands, Holstone Down, COMBE MARTIN, Devon, EX34 0PF. (£15.00)	01271 883463	625 477	3
			Saffron House Hotel, King Street, COMBE MARTIN, Devon, EX34 0BX. (£16.00)	01271 883521		3
*		*	Mrs A Waldon, Idlehour, Borough Road, COMBE MARTIN, Devon, EX34 0AN. (£11.00)	01271 883217		3
			Tourist Information Centre, Sea Cottage, Cross Street, COMBE MARTIN, Devon, EX34 0DH.	01271 883319		3
*	*	*	Mr & Mrs A G Furber, Slipway Cottage, 2 Hierns Lane, The Harbour, ILFRACOMBE, Devon, EX34 9EH. (£14.00)	01271 863035		4
*		*	Mrs M Howard, 2 Capstone Place, ILFRACOMBE, Devon, EX34 9TQ. (£12.50)	01271 865201		4
*	*	*	Mr & Mrs White, Trafalgar Hotel, Larkstone Terrace, Hillsborough Road, ILFRACOMBE, Devon, EX34 9NU. (£21.00)	01271 862145		4
*	*	*	Mr & Mrs Winearls, Norbury, Torrs Park, ILFRACOMBE, Devon, EX34 8AZ. (£15.50)	01271 863888		4

P	O	D	Name and Address	Telephone No.	Map Ref.	Section
			Tourist Information Centre, The Promenade, ILFRACOMBE, Devon, EX34 9BX.	01271 863001		4
*	*	*	Mrs Fran Nustedt, The Grampus Inn, LEE BAY, Nr Ilfracombe, Devon. (£16.00)	01271 862906		5
*		*	Lundy House Hotel, MORTEHOE, Devon. (£17.00)	01271 870372		5
*		*	Mrs A Braund, Clyst House, Rockfield Road, WOOLACOMBE, Devon, EX34 7DH. (£16.00)	01271 870220		6
*	*	*	Mr & Mrs S Bryant, Sunnyside Hotel, Sunnyside Road, WOOLACOMBE, Devon, EX34 7DG. (£16.00)	01271 870267		6
*	*	*	Mrs T Gyles, Ocean View, The Esplanade, WOOLACOMBE, Devon, EX34 7DJ. (£15.00)	01271 870359		6
*	*	*	Mr & Mrs H Riley, Camberley, Beach Road, WOOLACOMBE, Devon, EX34 7AA. (£16.00)	01271 870231	437 464	6
			Tourist Information Centre, Red Barn Café, Car Park, Barton Road, WOOLACOMBE, Devon.	01271 870553		6
*		*	Mr & Mrs C & R Gedling, West Winds Guest House, Moor Lane, CROYDE, Devon, EX33 1PA. (£21.00)	01271 890489		7
*		*	Mrs J Windsor, Chapel Farm, Hobbs Hill, CROYDE, Devon. (£18.00)	01271 890429	444 391	7
*	*	*	Mrs E Dale, 2 Links View, SAUNTON, Devon. (£12.50)	01271 812233		8
*	*	*	Mr & Mrs M & W Sargent, Alexander Brookdale Hotel, 62 South Street, BRAUNTON, Devon, EX33 2AN. (£18.50)	01271 812075		8
*	*	*	Mrs R C Saunders, Stockwell Lodge, 66 South Street, BRAUNTON, Devon. (£14.00)	01271 814338	486 361	8
*	*	*	Mrs Jean Watkins, North Cottage, 14 North Street, BRAUNTON, Devon, EX33 1AJ. (£12.50)	01271 812703	485 367	8
			Tourist Information Centre, Caen Street Car Park, BRAUNTON, Devon, EX33 1AA.	01271 816400		8
*	*	*	Mr & Mrs B & O Capp, Crossways, Braunton Road, BARNSTAPLE, Devon, EX31 1JY. (£13.50)	01271 79120	555 336	8
*	*	*	Newholme Guest House, Bickington Road, Sticklepath, BARNSTAPLE, Devon, EX31 2DB. (£14.00)	01271 72715		8
	*	*	Mrs L M Tucker, Enfield, Top of Sticklepath Hill, BARNSTAPLE, Devon, EX31 2DW. (£14.00)	01271 22949		8
			Tourist Information Centre, Devon Library, Tuly Street, BARNSTAPLE, Devon, EX31 1TY.	01271 47177		8

P	O	D	Name and Address	Telephone No.	Map Ref.	Section
*	*	*	Mrs D E George, Oakwood, 34 Yelland Road, FREMINGTON, Barnstaple, Devon, EX31 3DS. (£11.50)	01271 73884		9
*	*	*	Mrs J Garnsey, Ellerton, Glenburnie Road, BIDEFORD, Devon, EX39 2LW. (£13.50)	01237 473352		9
			Tourist Information Centre, Victoria Park, The Quay, BIDEFORD, Devon, EX39 2QQ.	01237 477676		9
*	*	*	Mount Hotel, Northdown Road, BIDEFORD, Devon, EX39 3LP. (£21.00)	01237 473748	479 269	9
*	*	*	Mrs M Cox, Riverside Guest House, 4 Marine Parade, APPLEDORE, Devon, EX39 1PJ. (£12.50)	01237 478649		9
*	*	*	Mr A R Milne, Skern Lodge, APPLEDORE, Devon, EX39 1NG. (£14.00)	01237 475992		9
*	*	*	Mr & Mrs M Federl, Locksley House, 1 Tower Street, NORTHAM, Devon, EX39 1JL. (£11.50)	01237 474885		9
*	*	*	Mrs J Johnson, 127 Bay View Road, NORTHAM, Devon. (£13.00)	01237 477088		9
*	*	*	Mrs Clegg, Mayfield, Avon Lane, WESTWARD HO!, Devon. (£12.50)	01237 477128		9
*		*	Mrs G P Ross, Beachside, Golf Links Road, WESTWARD HO!, Devon, EX39 1LH (£12.50)	01237 477021		9
*	*	*	Mr M Walker, Eversley, 1 Youngaton Road, WESTWARD HO!, Devon. (£13.50)	01237 471603		9
*	*	*	Mrs J Gould, The Old Mill, BUCKS MILL, Devon. (£14.00)	01237 431701		10
*	*	*	Mrs C Powell, Laburnum Cottage (opposite car park), BUCKS MILL, Nr. Bideford, Devon, EX39 5DY. (£13.50)	01237 431582		10
*	*	*	Mrs Curtis, Fuchsia Cottage, Burscott Lane, HIGHER CLOVELLY, Devon. (£12.00)	01237 431398	313 241	10
*		*	Mrs A Jewell, Burscott Farm, HIGHER CLOVELLY, Devon, EX39 5RR. (£12.50)	012374 431252	313 241	10
*	*	*	Mrs J Johns, Dyke Green Farm, HIGHER CLOVELLY, Nr. Bideford, Devon, EX39 5RU. (£14.50)	01237 431279	311 237	10
*	*	*	Mrs B May, Boat House, 148 Slerra Hill, HIGHER CLOVELLY, Devon, EX39 5ST. (£13.50)	01237 431209		10
*	*	*	Mrs P Vanstone, The Old Smithy, Slerra, HIGHER CLOVELLY, Devon, EX39 5ST. (£14.00)	01237 431202		10
*	*	*	Mrs L J Green, Donkey Shoe Cottage, 21 High Street, CLOVELLY, Devon. (£15.00)	01237 431601		10
*	*	*	The New Inn, CLOVELLY, Devon. (£17.00)	01237 431303		10

P	O	D	Name and Address	Telephone No.	Map Ref.	Section
*	*	*	Mrs Y Heard, West Titchberry Farm, HARTLAND POINT, Hartland, Devon, EX39 6AU. (£12.50)	01237 441287	242 272	11
		*	Mrs G Heard, Ekiya, 15 Brimacombe Road, HARTLAND, Devon. (£11.00)	01237 441539		11
*	*	*	Mr & Mrs Johns, Hartland Quay Hotel, HARTLAND, Devon, EX39 6DU. (£19.00)	01237 441371		11
*	*	*	Mr & Mrs D Mace, Lower Hardisworthy, Hardisworthy, HARTLAND, Devon, EX39 6ER. (£15.00)	01237 441850	228 204	11
*	*	*	Mrs B Slee, Homeleigh, Stoke, HARTLAND, Devon, EX39 6DU (on coast path). (£14.50)	01237 441465		11
*	*	*	Mrs B Downs, Strawberry Water, WELCOMBE MOUTH, Devon, EX39 6HL. (£10.00)	01288 331403		12

NORTH CORNWALL

P	O	D	Name and Address	Telephone No.	Map Ref.	Section
*	*	*	Mrs D Cholwill, Darzle Farm, Woodford, MORWENSTOW, Bude, Cornwall. (£15.00)	01288 331222	221 140	12
*	*	*	Mrs I Heard, Dene Farm, MORWENSTOW, Bude, Cornwall, EX23 9SL. (£15.00)	01288 331330	226 145	12
*	*	*	Mrs M C Heywood, Cornakey Farm, MORWENSTOW, Cornwall, EX23 9SS. (£14.00)	01288 331260		12
*	*	*	Mrs S A Trevin, Lower Northcott Farm, POUGHILL, Bude, Cornwall. (£15.00)	01288 352350		12
*	*	*	Mrs B Dunstan, Strands, Stibb, BUDE, Cornwall, EX23 9HW. (£13.00)	01288 353514		12
*	*	*	Mrs D Flanagan, Statton Gardens, Cott Hill, Stratton, BUDE, Cornwall, EX23 9DN (will collect) (£17.00)	01288 352500	232 065	12
*	*	*	E & L Hatch, Seaview, 51 Killerton Road, BUDE, Cornwall, EX23 8EN. (£16.00)	01288 352665		12
*	*	*	Mrs G Hill, Corisande Hotel, 24 Downs View, BUDE, Cornwall, EX23 8RG. (£15.00)	01288 353474		12
*	*	*	Mr & Mrs P Kimpton, Kisauni, 4 Downs View, BUDE, Cornwall. (£12.00)	01288 352653		12
*		*	The Meva-Gwin Hotel, Upton, BUDE, Cornwall, EX23 0LY. (£18.00)	01288 352347		12
*	*	*	Mrs Mills, Wyvern House, 7 Downs View, BUDE, Cornwall, EX23 8BF. (£13.00)	01288 352205		12
*		*	Mornish Hotel, Summerleaze Crescent, BUDE, Cornwall, EX23 8HJ. (£18.50)	01288 352972	221 140	12
*	*	*	Mr M E Payne, Pencarrol Guest House, 21 Downs View, BUDE, Cornwall, EX23 8RF. (£14.00)	01288 352478		12
*	*	*	Mrs M Stock, 8 Downs View, BUDE, Cornwall, EX23 8RF. (£12.00)	01288 355059		12
*	*	*	Mr & Mrs J Thorne, The Farthings, 4 Killerton Road, BUDE, Cornwall, EX23 8EL. (£10.00)	01288 355310		12

P	O	D	Name and Address	Telephone No.	Map Ref.	Section
			Tourist Information Centre, Crescent Car Park, BUDE, Cornwall, EX23 8LE	01288 354240		12
*	*	*	Bay View Inn, Marine Drive, WIDEMOUTH BAY, Cornwall, EX23 0AW. (£12.00)	01288 361273	201 028	13
*		*	Mr Marks, Penhalt Farm, WIDEMOUTH BAY, Cornwall. (£12.00)	01288 361210		13
*	*	*	Mr & Mrs J & A Connell, Gunnedah House, CRACKINGTON HAVEN, Nr. Bude, Cornwall, EX23 0JZ. (£14.00)	01840 230265	144 966	13
*		*	Mr & Mrs J Cooper, Coombe Barton Inn, CRACKINGTON HAVEN, Cornwall, EX23 0JG. (£15.00)	01840 230345	143 968	13
*	*	*	Mrs R Crocker, Tregather, CRACKINGTON HAVEN, Nr. Bude, Cornwall, EX23 0LQ. (£14.00)	018403 667		13
*	*	*	Mrs E A Redman, 8 Penkenna Close, CRACKINGTON HAVEN, Cornwall, EX23 0PF. (£14.00)	01840 230413	155 956	13
*	*	*	Mrs L Ruff, Nancemellan, CRACKINGTON HAVEN, Cornwall, EX23 0NN. (£15.00)	01840 230283	150 968	13

YOUTH HOSTELS BOSCASTLE, TINTAGEL, PADSTOW, NEWQUAY, PERRANPORTH –
SEE Y.H.A. SECTION PAGE

P	O	D	Name and Address	Telephone No.	Map Ref.	Section
*	*	*	Mr & Mrs Fillery, Forrabury House, Forrabury Common, BOSCASTLE, Cornwall, PL35 0DJ. (£14.00)	01840 250469		14
*	*	*	Mr & Mrs G Mee, Bottreaux House Hotel, BOSCASTLE, Cornwall, PL35 0BG. (£20.00)	01840 250231	100 906	14
*	*	*	Mrs C Nicholls, Trerosewill Farm, Paradise, BOSCASTLE, Cornwall, PL35 0DL. (£15.00)	01840 250545	096 905	14
*		*	Tolcarne House Hotel, Tintagel Road, BOSCASTLE, Cornwall. (£18.00)	01840 250654	In Boscastle	14
*	*	*	Mrs M Webber, Myrtle Cottage, Fore Street, BOSCASTLE, Cornwall, PL35 0AX. (£12.50)	01840 250245	In village	14
*	*	*	Mr T A Read, Trevillett Mill Trout Farm, ROCKY VALLEY, Tintagel, Cornwall, PL34 0BB. (£15.00)	01840 770564	075 892	15
*		*	Mrs A Jones, Grange Cottage, BOSSINEY, Tintagel, Cornwall, PL34 0AX. (£14.00)	01840 770487	065 887	15
*	*	*	L N Leeds, Willapark Manor Hotel, BOSSINEY, Tintagel, Cornwall, PL34 0BA. (£23.00)	01840 770782		15
*		*	Bosayne Guest House, Atlantic Road, TINTAGEL, Cornwall, PL34 0DE. (£14.00)	01840 770514		15
	*	*	Mr & Mrs I Pinchen, Ocean View, 4 King Arthur's Terrace, TINTAGEL, Cornwall. (£11.00)	01840 770675		15

P	O	D	Name and Address	Telephone No.	Map Ref.	Section
*		*	Mr & Mrs D E Wilson, The Riggs, Bossiney Road, TINTAGEL, Cornwall, PL34 0AH. (£13.00)	01840 770427	058 884	15
*	*	*	Port Gaverne Hotel, PORT GAVERNE, Port Isaac, Cornwall, PL29 3SQ. (£43.00)	01208 880244		16
*	*	*	Mrs K Castle, Dunoon Guest House, 12 Tintagel Terrace, PORT ISAAC, Cornwall, PL29 3SE. (£12.00)	01208 880383	998 810	16
*	*	*	Mrs J Corrigan, The Homestead, Tintagel Terrace, PORT ISAAC, Cornwall. (£12.50)	01208 880064		16
*		*	Mrs G Hooper, Gwel Arvor, Tintagel Terrace, PORT ISAAC, Cornwall, PL29 3SE. (£11.50)	01208 880404		16
*	*	*	Ms J Mann, The Castle Rock Hotel, PORT ISAAC, Cornwall, PL29 3SB. (£30.00)	01208 880300		16
*	*	*	Old School Hotel, Guest House and Restaurant, PORT ISAAC, Cornwall. (£16.00)	01208 880721	996 808	16
*	*	*	St Andrews Hotel, 18 The Terrace, PORT ISAAC, Cornwall, PL29 3SG. (£16.00)	01208 880240	001 809	16
*	*	*	Mrs M Pashley, Pentire View Guest House, POLZEATH, Cornwall, PL27 6TB. (£13.00)	01208 862484		17
*	*	*	Mr M Martin, Silvermead, ROCK, Wadebridge, Cornwall, PL27 6LB. (£15.00)	01208 862425		18
*		*	Roskarnon House Hotel, ROCK, Nr. Wadebridge, Cornwall, PL27 6LD. (£20.00)	01208 862329		18
*		*	Mr & Mrs E Champion, 8 Treverbyn Road, PADSTOW, Cornwall, PL28 8DW. (£15.00)	01841 532551		18
*	*	*	Mrs C Gidlow, Cross House Hotel, Church Street, PADSTOW, Cornwall, PL28 8BG. (£18.00)	01841 532391		18
	*		Mrs E McGregor, 2 Dennis Road, PADSTOW, Cornwall, PL28 8DD. (£14.50)	01841 532767		18
*		*	Mrs L Mills, Ellan Gowan, 34 Dennis Road, PADSTOW, Cornwall. (£13.50)	01841 533361		18
	*		Mrs M Morcom, "Lanwednok", 8 Egerton Road, PADSTOW, Cornwall, PL28. (£15.00)	01841 532539		18
			Tourist Information Centre, North Quay, PADSTOW, Cornwall, PL28 8AF.	01841 533449		18
*		*	Mrs J Ball, Gwel-an-Nans, Homer Park Road, TREVONE, Cornwall, PL28 8QU. (£15.00)	01841 520769		19
*		*	Mrs S Hamilton, Trevone Bay Hotel, TREVONE, Padstow, Cornwall, PL28 8QS. (£19.00)	01841 520243	892 755	19

P	O	D	Name and Address	Telephone No.	Map Ref.	Section
*	*	*	Treyarnon Bay Hotel, TREYARNON BAY, Padstow, Cornwall, PL28 8DD. (£10.00)	01841 520235	860 740	20
*		*	Mr B Coombes, Bay House Hotel, PORTHCOTHAN BAY, Padstow, Cornwall. (£15.00)	01841 520472		20
*	*	*	Mr & Mrs J M Shadbolt, Trelooan, PORTHCOTHAN, Padstow, Cornwall, PL28 8LS. (£14.00)	01841 521158	858 716	20
*		*	Mrs L Bennett, The Merrymoor, MAWGAN PORTH, Cornwall, TR8 4BA. (£15.00)	01637 860258		21
*	*	*	Mrs C Lambert, Double K Hotel, Trevarrian, MAWGAN PORTH, Cornwall, TR8 4AQ. (£14.00)	01637 860422		21
*	*	*	Mr & Mrs C Robinson, Sea Vista Hotel, MAWGAN PORTH, Cornwall, TR8 4AL. (£15.00)	01637 860276		21
*	*	*	Tanzarra Villa, Tredragon Road, MAWGAN PORTH, Cornwall, TR7 4DQ. (£12.50)	01637 860628		21
*		*	White Lodge Hotel, MAWGAN PORTH, Cornwall, TR8 4BN. (£18.50)	01637 860512		21
*	*	*	Mrs A Atkinson, Springvale Guest House, 112 Henver Road, NEWQUAY, Cornwall, TR7 3EQ. (£13.00)	01637 873857	830 620	21
*	*	*	D & A Connor, Belair Guest House, 28 Edgcumbe Avenue, NEWQUAY, Cornwall, TR7 2NH. (£13.00)	01637 876503		21
*		*	Corisande Manor Hotel, Riverside Avenue., Pentire, NEWQUAY, Cornwall, TR7 1PL. (£20.00)	01637 872042	794 613	21
*	*	*	Crantock Plains Farmhouse, Cubert, NEWQUAY, Cornwall, TR8 5PH. (£15.00)	01637 830253		21
*	*	*	S R Harper, Chichester, 14 Bay View, NEWQUAY, Cornwall, TR7 2LR. (£11.00)	01637 874216		21
*	*	*	Mr & Mrs A Hart, Portafino Hotel, 56 Penhallow Road, Porth, NEWQUAY, Cornwall, TR7 3BY. (£15.00)	01637 875589	829 626	21
*		*	Mrs S Schofield, Hemick Lodge, 33 Pentire Ave., NEWQUAY Cornwall, TR7 1PB. (£12.50)	01637 872592	795 614	21
*	*	*	St Mawes Hotel, Springfield Road, NEWQUAY, Cornwall, TR7 1RT. (£14.00)	01637 872754		21
*		*	Mr G Stevenson, Hotel Trevalsa, Watergate Road, Porth, NEWQUAY, Cornwall, TR7 3LX. (£18.00)	01637 873336		21
*	*	*	Tregurrian Hotel, Watergate Bay, NEWQUAY, Cornwall, TR8 4AB. (£18.00)	01637 860280	844 649	21

P	O	D	Name and Address	Telephone No. 01637	Map Ref.	Section
			Tourist Information Centre, Municipal Offices, Marcus Hill, NEWQUAY, Cornwall, TR7 1BD.	01637 871345		21
*		*	Mr & Mrs Eyles, Crantock Bay Hotel, West Pentire, CRANTOCK, Cornwall, TR8 5SE. (£29.00)	01637 830229	777 607	22
*	*	*	Mr & Mrs Somerville, The Goose Rock Hotel, West Pentire, CRANTOCK, Cornwall. (£19.00)	01637 830755	776 607	22
*	*	*	Sue Wrigley, Tregenna House, West Pentire Road, CRANTOCK, Cornwall, TR8 5RZ. (£12.50)	01637 830222	787 604	22
*	*	*	Mrs Crofts, Tremore, Liskey Hill Cres., PERRANPORTH, Cornwall. (£15.00)	01872 573537		23
*	*	*	Mr & Mrs J Wells, 44 Tywarnhayle Road, PERRANPORTH, Cornwall, TR6 0DX. (£11.00)	01872 572380		23
			Tourist Information Centre, Beiners Arms Hotel, PERRANPORTH, Cornwall.	01872 573368		23
*	*	*	Mrs J Ball, 15 Durning Road, ST AGNES, Cornwall, TR5 0UP. (£12.00)	01872 552532	717 502	24
*	*	*	Mrs Gill-Carey, Penkerris, Penwinnick Road, ST AGNES, Cornwall. (£13.50)	01872 552262	722 503	24
*	*	*	Mrs Glover, Beach Cottage, Quay Road, ST AGNES, Cornwall. (£13.00)	01872 553802	722 513	24
*	*	*	Mrs Treleaven, Driftwood Spars Hotel, Trevaunance Cove, ST AGNES, Cornwall, TR5 0RT. (£27.00)	01872 552428	722 514	24
*	*	*	Mrs G Van Leeuwen, Chy Todden, "Frying Dutchman", Quay Road, ST AGNES, Cornwall, TR5 0RY (on cliff path). (£19.00)	01872 552664	721 514	24
*		*	Ms V Parkinson, Buzby View, Forthvean Road, PORTHTOWAN, Cornwall, TR4 8AY. (£14.00)	01209 891178		25
*	*	*	Mrs Benson, Benson's, 1 The Hillside, PORTREATH, Cornwall, TR16 4LL. (£25.00)	01209 842534	659 451	26
*		*	Glenfeadon House Hotel, PORTREATH, Cornwall, TR16 4JV. (£17.00)	01209 842650	657 454	26
*	*	*	C J & J E Healan, Cliff House, The Square, PORTREATH, Cornwall, TR16 4LB. (£15.00)	01209 842008		26
*	*	*	Mr & Mrs R Pattinson, Sycamore Lodge, Primrose Terrace, PORTREATH, Cornwall, TR16 4JS. (£16.00)	01209 842784	661 451	26
*	*	*	Mrs M Symonds, Suhaili, 14 Forth-an-Nance, PORTREATH, Cornwall, TR16 4NQ. (£14.00)	01209 842110	656 453	26
*	*	*	Mrs A Ellis, Vellynsaundry, Pendarves, CAMBORNE, Cornwall. (Will collect & deliver from path) (£11.00)	01209 712983	639 381	26

P	O	D	Name and Address	Telephone No.	Map Ref.	Section
*	*	*	Calize Country House, Prosper Hill, GWITHIAN, Cornwall, TR27 5BW. (£15.00)	01736 753268	589 409	27
*	*	*	Mrs L Davies, Nanterrow Farm, GWITHIAN, Cornwall, TR27 5BP. (Will pick up & return) (£13.00)	01209 712282	599 412	27
*	*	*	Mr & Mrs D Eddy, Orchard Close, 3 Church Town Road, GWITHIAN, Nr. Hayle, Cornwall. (£13.00)	01736 753077		27
*	*	*	Mrs A Cooper, 54 Penpol Terrace, HAYLE, Cornwall, TR27 4BQ. (£15.00)	01736 752855		27
*	*	*	White Hart Hotel, 10 Foundry Square, HAYLE, Cornwall, TR27 4HQ. (£25.00)	01736 752322		27
	*	*	Mr & Mrs W Batty, The Grey Mullet, 2 Bunkers Hill, ST IVES, Cornwall. (£15.00)	01736 796635		28
*		*	Mrs King, Carlill, 9 Porthminster Terrace, ST IVES, Cornwall, TR26 2DQ. (£13.00)	01736 796738		28
	*	*	Mr & Mrs D Mason, Kandahar, 11 The Warren, ST IVES, Cornwall, TR26 2EA. (£17.50)	01736 796183		28
*	*	*	Mrs Millin, Lynmar, 4 The Terrace, ST IVES, Cornwall, TR26 2BL. (£13.00)	01736 794152		28
			Tourist Information Centre, The Guildhall, Street an Pol, ST IVES, Cornwall, TR26 2DT.	01736 796297		28
*		*	Mrs Berryman, Treen Farm, Gurnards Road, ZENNOR, St Ives, Cornwall, TR26 3DE. (£12.50)	01736 796932	436 377	29
*	*	*	Boswednack Manor, ZENNOR, St Ives, Cornwall, TR26 3DD. (£14.00)	01736 794183	442 377	29
*	*	*	Mrs L A Hawkins, Carnelloe House, ZENNOR, St Ives, Cornwall, TR26 3DB. (£18.50)	01736 798946		29
*	*	*	N I Mann, Trewey Farm, ZENNOR, St Ives, Cornwall. (£14.00)	01736 796936	454 384	29
*		*	Pennance Farm, ZENNOR, Nr. St Ives, Cornwall. (£12.50)	01736 796972		29
*		*	Mrs A B Prowse, Trewey Vean Farm, ZENNOR, St Ives, Cornwall. (£14.00)	01736 796919	454 384	29
*	*	*	Mr & Mrs C Arms, The Old Smugglers Haunt Tea Rooms, PENDEEN, Cornwall, TR19 7SG. (£14.00)	01736 788310		29
*	*	*	Mrs Bailey, Trewellard Manor Farm, PENDEEN, Cornwall. (£15.00)	01736 788526	375 339	29
*	*	*	Mrs B Brooke, Enys, Lighthouse Road, PENDEEN, Penzance, Cornwall, TR19 7ED. (£16.00)	01736 787143	380 358	29
*	*	*	Mrs J Davey, Pendeen Manor, PENDEEN, Cornwall, TR19 7ED. (£15.00)	01736 788753		29

P	O	D	Name and Address	Telephone No.	Map Ref.	Section
*		*	Mr & Mrs T Dymond, The Old Count House, Boscaswell Down, PENDEEN, Near Penzance, Cornwall. (£13.00)	01736 788058		29
*	*	*	The Radjel Inn, PENDEEN, Cornwall, TR19 7DS. (£12.50)	01736 788446	385 344	29
*	*	*	Mrs E A Scambler, Bosigran Farm, PENDEEN, Cornwall, TR20 7YX. (£13.50)	01736 796940	426 370	29
*	*	*	Mrs C Stone, 16 Levant Road, Trewellard, PENDEEN, Cornwall, TR19 7SU. (£12.00)	01736 787984		29
	*		Mrs J Cargeeg, Manor Farm, BOTALLACK, Cornwall, TR19 7QG. (£16.00)	01736 788525	328 370	30
*	*	*	Mrs E Lawry, Llawnroc, 1 Truthwall Villa, BOTALLACK, Cornwall. (£12.00)	01736 788814		30
	*		Boswedden House Hotel, Cape Cornwall, ST JUST, Penzance, Cornwall. (£18.00)	01736 788733	360 318	30
*	*	*	Mr & Mrs B Collins, Cape House, Cape Cornwall, ST JUST, Nr. Penzance, Cornwall, TR19 7NN. (£15.00)	01736 787112		30
*		*	Mrs A D Eddy, Trethewes, Carrallack Terrace, ST JUST, Penzance, Cornwall, TR19 7LP. (£14.00)	01736 788528		30
*		*	Mr & Mrs J R Hartley, Bosavern House, ST JUST, Penzance, Cornwall, TR19 7RD. (£13.75)	01736 788301	371 305	30
	*		Mr & Mrs R Lee, Boscean Country Hotel, Boswedden Road, ST JUST, Cornwall, TR19 7QP. (£20.00)	01736 788748		30
	*		Mr & Mrs P Michelmore, 2 Fore Street, ST JUST, Nr. Penzance, Cornwall. (£12.50)	01736 787784	371 313	30
	*	*	Mr & Mrs D Gallie, Polwyn Cottage, Old Coastguard Row, SENNEN COVE, Cornwall, TR19 7DA. (£13.50)	01736 871349	350 264	31
*	*	*	Old Success Inn, SENNEN COVE, Cornwall, TR19 7DG. (£24.00)	01736 871232		31
	*	*	A & A Rees, Myrtle Cottage, Old Coastguard Road, SENNEN COVE, Penzance, Cornwall. (£13.50)	01736 871698	351 262	31
*	*	*	Mrs Flumm, Lyonesse Guest House, Land's End, SENNEN, Cornwall, TR19 7AD. (£12.50)	01736 871207	357 257	31
*		*	D Wedlake, Sennen Cove Hotel, Marias Lane, SENNEN, Near Penzance, Cornwall. (£17.50)	01736 871275		31

SOUTH CORNWALL

YOUTH HOSTELS PENZANCE, HELSTON, FALMOUTH, ST AUSTELL – SEE Y.H.A. SECTION PAGE

P	O	D	Name and Address	Telephone No.	Map Ref.	Section
*	*	*	Mr & Mrs P Christ, Sea View House, The Valley, PORTHCURNO, Penzance, Cornwall TR19 6JX. (£14.50)	01736 810638	382 230	32

P	O	D	Name and Address	Telephone No.	Map Ref.	Section
*	*	*	Mr & Mrs J Ring, Corniche, Trebehor, PORTHCURNO, Cornwall, TR19 6LX. (Will pick up). (£12.00)	01736 871685	375 243	32
*		*	Mr & Mrs Thomas, Grey Gables, PORTHCURNO, Cornwall, TR19 6JT. (£15.00)	01736 810421		32
*	*	*	Mrs A Jilbert, Penver House Farm, TREEN, Penzance, Cornwall. (£15.00)	01736 810778		33
*	*	*	Mr & Mrs B Richards, Tremeneth Hotel, LAMORNA, Nr. Penzance, Cornwall, TR19 6XL. (£15.00)	01736 731367		33
*	*	*	Mrs Bartlett, Renovelle, 6 The Parade, MOUSEHOLE, Penzance, Cornwall, TR19 6PN. (£11.50)	01736 731258		34
*	*	*	The Lobster Pot, MOUSEHOLE, Cornwall, TR19 6QX. (£22.50)	01736 731251	469 263	34
*	*	*	Miss R Knubley, Alexandra Hotel, Seafront, PENZANCE, Cornwall, TR18 4NX. (£20.00)	01736 62644		34
*	*	*	Mrs G Ash, Torre Vene, Lescudjack Terrace, PENZANCE, Cornwall, TR18 3AE. (£14.00)	01736 64103		34
*	*	*	Tarbert Hotel, Clarence Street, PENZANCE, Cornwall, TR18 2NU. (£22.50)	01736 63758		34
			Tourist Information Centre, Station Road, PENZANCE, Cornwall, TR18 2NF.	01736 62207		34
*	*	*	Mrs I S Glover, Anneth Lowen, Leys Lane, MARAZION, Cornwall. (£12.00)	01736 710211		35
*		*	The Kings Arms, MARAZION, Cornwall, TR17 0AP. (£12.50)	01736 710291		35
*	*	*	Mrs M Foy, Mzima, Penlee Close, PRAA SANDS, Nr. Penzance, Cornwall. (£12.00)	01736 763856		36
*		*	Mrs Jennings, Boslowen-Mor, Castle Drive, PRAA SANDS, Cornwall, TR20 9TF. (£11.50)	01736 762223		36
*	*	*	Mrs C Cookson, Pentre, Peverell Terrace, PORTHLEVEN, Cornwall, TR13 9DZ. (£14.00)	01326 574493	630 255	37
*	*	*	Mrs K Cox, Quayside Cottage, 12 Harbour View, PORTHLEVEN, Cornwall, TR13 9JN. (£15.00)	01326 562200		37
*	*	*	Mr Hallam, Seefar, Peverell Terrace, PORTHLEVEN, Cornwall. (£12.00)	01326 573778		37
*	*	*	Ms M Kelymack, An Modros Hotel, Peverell Terrace, PORTHLEVEN, Cornwall, TR13 9BZ. (£14.50)	01326 562236		37
		*	Tye Rock Hotel, Loe Bar Road, PORTHLEVEN, Cornwall, TR13 9EW. (£26.25)	01326 572695		37

P	O	D	Name and Address	Telephone No.	Map Ref.	Section
*	*	*	S A Archer, Redannack Bungalow, Lender Lane, MULLION, Cornwall, TR12 7HS. (£13.50)	01326 240936		38
*	*	*	Mrs I Clarke, Trematon, Polurrian Cliff Road, MULLION, Cornwall, TR12 7EW (on the path). (£12.50)	01326 240344		38
*	*	*	Pauline Story, Criggan Mill, MULLION COVE, Cornwall, TR12 7EU. (£12.00)	01326 240496	671 178	38
*	*	*	Mr & Mrs M Wood, Trenance Barton, MULLION, Cornwall, TR12 7HB. (£13.50)	01326 240893	672 184	38
	*		Mrs P Hocking, Bayview, Cross Common, THE LIZARD, Helston, Cornwall, TR12 7PD. (£12.50)	01326 290369	707 126	39
*		*	Mr & Mrs S Kilmister, Parc Brawse House, Penmenner Road, THE LIZARD, Helston, Cornwall, TR12 7NR. (£13.00)	01326 290466	702 122	39
	*		Mrs G Rowe, Trethvas Farm, THE LIZARD, Helston, Cornwall, TR12 7AR. (£13.50)	01326 290720	709 136	39
*	*	*	Mrs K Thirlaway, Green Cottage, THE LIZARD, Cornwall, TR12 7NZ. (£12.00)	01326 290099		39
*	*	*	Caerthillian Farmhouse, LIZARD, Near Helston, Cornwall, TR12 7NX. (£14.00)	01326 290596		39
*		*	Mrs I Sowden, The Most Southerly House, LIZARD POINT, Cornwall, TR12 7NU. (£13.00)	01326 290300	702 115	39
*		*	Mrs L Johnson, Moorlands, Prazegooth Lane, CADGWITH, Nr Helston, Cornwall, TR12 7LB. (£15.00)	01326 290932		40
*		*	Mrs T Carey, Tamarisk Cottage, COVERACK, Helston, Cornwall. (£13.50)	01326 280638		40
*	*	*	Mr P Cheze-Brown, The Croft, North Corner, COVERACK, Cornwall, TR12 6TF. (£13.50)	01326 280387	783 187	40
*	*	*	Mrs E Daw, Bakery Cottage, COVERACK, Nr Helston, Cornwall. (£13.00)	01326 280474		40
*	*	*	Gallen-Treath Guest House, P Peters, PORTHALLOW, St Keverne, Cornwall. (£16.50)	01326 280400		41
*	*	*	Mrs R Peters, Valley View, PORTHALLOW, St. Keverne, Cornwall, TR12 6PN. (£13.50)	01326 280596	796 232	41
*	*	*	Mrs P Julian, Landrivick Farm, MANACCAN, Near Helston, Cornwall. (£16.00)	01326 231249		41
*		*	Tregildry Hotel, Gillan, MANACCAN, Nr Helston, Cornwall, TR12 6HG. (£25.00)	01326 231378		41
*	*	*	Mrs J Chambers, Heronsway, Orchard Lane, HELFORD, Cornwall, TR12 6LA. (£15.00)	01326 231424	755 260	41

P	O	D	Name and Address	Telephone No.	Map Ref.	Section
*	*	*	Mrs Spike, Carwinion Vean, Grove Hill, MAWNAN SMITH, Near Falmouth, Cornwall, TR11 5ER. (£17.50)	01326 250513		42
*	*	*	Dr & Mrs K G Leach, St Petroc, The Avenue, TRURO, Cornwall, TR1 1HR. (will pick up from and return to coast path). (£14.00)	01872 70768		42
*	*	*	Mrs Bryant, Ambleside, 9 Marlborough Road, FALMOUTH, Cornwall, TR11 3LP. (£14.00)	01326 319630		42
*	*	*	The Grove Hotel, Grove Place, FALMOUTH, Cornwall, TR11 4AV. (£20.00)	01326 319577		42
*		*	Mr & Mrs D & M Siderfin, Bradgate Guest House, 4 Florence, Place, FALMOUTH, Cornwall. (£14.00)	01326 314108		42
*	*	*	Mr J T Trezise, Selwood Cottage, 38 Melvill Road, FALMOUTH, Cornwall, TR11 4DQ. (£14.00)	01326 314135	811 320	42
*		*	Mrs Watmore, Rosemary Hotel, Gyllyngvase Terrace, FALMOUTH, Cornwall. (£16.00)	01326 314669	810 318	42
			Tourist Information Centre 28 Killigrew Street, FALMOUTH, Cornwall, TR11 3PN.	01326 312300		42
		*	Braganza, Grove Hill, ST MAWES, Cornwall. (£18.00)	01326 270281	847 333	43
*	*	*	Mrs D Palmer, Penhallow Coombe Farm, Treworlas, Ruan High Lanes, ST MAWES, Cornwall, TR2 5LR. (£12.00)	01872 501105		43
	*	*	Mrs A Palmer, Trenestrall Farm, Ruan High Lanes, PORTSCATHO, Cornwall (will pick up from path). (£13.00)	01872 501259	886 399	44
*	*	*	Mr & Mrs R Pooler, Tregerein Guest House, PORTSCATHO, Cornwall, TR2 5HT. (£14.00)	01872 580336		44
	*	*	Mrs J Smith, 4 Parc An Dillon, PORTSCATHO, Cornwall, TR2 5DU. (£16.00)	01872 580310		44
*	*	*	Mr & Mrs R Foley, St Petroc, PORTLOE, Cornwall, TR2 5RA. (£12.50)	01872 501143		45
*	*	*	Mrs C Holdsworth, Tregain Tea Room, The Post Office, PORTLOE, Truro, Cornwall, TR2 5QU. (£17.50)	01872 501252		45
*	*	*	Mr J H Gregory, Llawnroc Inn, GORRAN HAVEN, Cornwall, PL26 6NU. (£18.00)	01726 843461		47
*	*	*	Gill Mott, Piggy Pantry, The Willows, GORRAN HAVEN, St. Austell, Cornwall. (£16.00)	01726 843545		47
*	*	*	Mr & Mrs D Youlden, Steep House, PORTMELLON COVE, Mevagissey, Cornwall, PL26 6TQ. (£16.00)	01726 843732	017 441	48

P	O	D	Name and Address	Telephone No.	Map Ref.	Section
*	*	*	Ms J Connolly, Mandalay Hotel, School Hill, MEVAGISSEY, Cornwall, PL26 6TQ. (£15.00)	01726 842435		48
*	*	*	Mrs Harris, Polvellan School Hill, MEVAGISSEY, Cornwall, PL26 6TG. (£16.00)	01726 842197		48
*		*	A H Lawrence, Tregoron Guest House, Cliff Street, MEVAGISSEY, Cornwall, PL26 6QW. (£15.00)	01726 842319	016 441	48
*		*	Mrs J Rowe, Rosedale, Valley Park, Tregoney Hill, MEVAGISSEY, Cornwall, PL26 6RS. (£14.15)	01726 842769		48
*		*	Mrs M Bainbridge, Polrudden Farm, PENTEWAN, Nr Mevagissey, Cornwall, PL26 6BJ. (£16.00)	01726 843213	025 475	48
	*	*	Mrs Anderson, Treveglos, Church Road, CHARLESTOWN, Cornwall, PL25 3NS. (£14.00)	01726 61424		49
*	*	*	Mr M I Christie, T'Gallants Guest House, 6 Charlestown Road, CHARLESTOWN, Cornwall, PL25 3NJ. (£17.00)	01726 70203		49
*	*	*	Ms S Mathieson 11 Coastguard Terrace, CHARLESTOWN, Nr. St. Austell, Cornwall. (£12.00)	01726 72828	039 516	49
*	*	*	Porth Avallen Hotel, Sea Road, Carlyon Bay, CHARLESTOWN, Nr. St. Austell, Cornwall, PL25 3SG. (£36.00)	01726 812802		49
*	*	*	Rashleigh Arms Hotel, CHARLESTOWN, St. Austell, Cornwall. (£24.00)	01726 73635		49
	*	*	Mrs B D Burgess, 55 Polmear Road, PAR, Cornwall, PL24 2AW. (£10.00)	01726 812967	086 535	50
			Tourist Information Centre, The Post Office, 4 Custom House Hill, FOWEY, Cornwall, PL23 1AA.	01726 833616		51
*	*	*	Mrs J Rowledge, Trevanion Guest House, 70 Lostwithiel Street, FOWEY, Cornwall, PL23 1BQ. (£14.00)	01726 832602		51
*	*	*	Mr & Mrs D Turner, Topsides, The Esplanade, FOWEY, Cornwall, PL23 1HZ. (£15.00)	01726 833715	124 516	51
*	*	*	Mrs B Blamey, Holly House, Fore Street, POLRUAN, Cornwall, PL23 1PU. (£13.50)	01726 870478		52
*	*	*	Mrs P Moore, Chyavallon, Landaviddy Lane, POLPERRO, Cornwall, PL13 2RT (centre of village). (£14.00)	01503 72788		52
*	*	*	Mrs C Talling, Lansallos Barton Farm, Lansallos, POLPERRO, Cornwall, PL13 2PU. (£12.00)	01503 72192		52
*	*	*	Mr & Mrs M Westcott, Penhallow-on-Brent, Talland Hill, POLPERRO, Cornwall, PL13 2RY (300 yards from path). (£16.00)	01503 72689		52l

P	O	D	Name and Address	Telephone No.	Map Ref.	Section
*	*	*	Mrs Matthews, Steward House, TALLAND BAY, Nr. Looe, Cornwall, PL13 2JA. (£15.00)	01503 72282		53
*	*	*	Mr M Neaves, Schooner Point, 1 Trelawney Terrace, WEST LOOE, Cornwall, PL13 2AG. (£12.00)	01503 262670		53
			Tourist Information Centre, The Guildhall, Fore Street, LOOE, Cornwall, PL13 1AA.	01503 262072		53
*	*	*	Mr J Chapman, Woodlands, St Martins Road, EAST LOOE, Cornwall, PL13 1LP. (£18.00)	01503 264405	255 535	53
*	*	*	Marwinthy Guest House, East Cliff, EAST LOOE, Cornwall, PL13 1DE. (£15.00)	01503 264382	256 533	53
*	*	*	Mrs M'Queen, Penvith Barns, ST MARTIN-BY-LOOE, Cornwall, PL13 1NZ. (£17.00)	01503 240772	283 541	54
*	*	*	Mrs A White, Blue Haven Hotel, Looe Hill, SEATON, Cornwall, PL11 3JQ. (£13.50)	01503 250310		54
*	*	*	Mr & Mrs P Di Bello, The Inn on the Shore, DOWNDERRY, Cornwall, PL11 3JY. (£10.00)	01503 250210		54
*		*	Mrs A J Harvey, The Bungalow, Cliff Road, CRAFTHOLE, Nr. Torpoint, Cornwall, PL11 3BY. (£15.00)	01503 30334	355 541	54
*	*	*	Mr & Mrs P Ridpath, Fir Cottage, Lower Tregantle, CRAFTHOLE, Cornwall, PL11 3AL (1/4 mile from fort). (£15.00)	01752 822626		54
*	*	*	C Collins, Avon House, Garrett Street, CAWSAND, Cornwall, PL10 1DB. (£12.00)	01752 822229	435 503	55
*	*	*	Mr & Mrs A Fidler, Rame Barton, Rame, CAWSAND, Nr. Torpoint, Cornwall, PL10 1LG. (£15.00)	01752 822789	425 492	55
*	*	*	Halfway House Inn, Fore Street, Cawsand Bay, KINGSAND, Cornwall, PL10 1NA. (£19.50)	01752 822279	435 505	55
*	*	*	Ms T Williams, Westcroft, Market Street, KINGSAND, Cornwall, PL10 1NE. (12ft from beach). (£12.50)	01752 823216		55
*	*	*	Mrs G Wood, Friary Manor Hotel, Maker Heights, KINGSAND, Nr. Mt. Edgcumbe Pk, Cornwall, PL10 1JB. (£18.00)	01752 822112	443 518 (shown as Vicarage)	55

SOUTH DEVON

YOUTH HOSTELS PLYMOUTH, BRIXHAM, SEATON – SEE Y.H.A. SECTION PAGE

P	O	D	Name and Address	Telephone No.	Map Ref.	Section
*	*	*	Mrs A Coon, Berkeley's of St. James G.H., 4 St James Place East, The Hoe, PLYMOUTH, Devon, PL1 3AS. (£15.00)	01752 221654		56
*	*	*	Kynance Hotel, 107/113 Citadel Road, The Hoe, PLYMOUTH, Devon, PL1 2RN. (£19.50)	01752 266821	544 481	56

P	O	D	Name and Address	Telephone No.	Map Ref.	Section
*	*	*	Mr & Mrs M H Preece, Rigsbys Guest House, 35 North Road East, PLYMOUTH, Devon, PL4 6AY. (£15.00)	01752 669161		56
*	*	*	Mrs J Turner, Rusty Anchor, 30 Grand Parade, West Hoe, PLYMOUTH, Devon, PL1 3DJ. (£12.00)	01752 663924		56
			Tourist Information Centre, Island House, 9 The Barbican, PLYMOUTH, Devon.	01752 264849/264851		56
*	*	*	Mrs Janet Rayne, The Boringdon Arms, TURNCHAPEL, Nr. Plymouth, Devon, PL9 9TQ. (£14.00)	01752 402053		56
*	*	*	Heybrook Bay Private Hotel, Beach Road, HEYBROOK BAY, Near Plymouth, Devon, PL9 0BS. (£16.00).	01752 862345		57
*	*	*	Mrs S Farrington, Bay Cottage, 150 Church Road, WEMBURY, Devon, PL7 0HR. (£21.00)	01752 862559	520 4856	57
*	*	*	Mrs J Cross, Maywood Cottage, Bridgend, NEWTON FERRERS, Devon, PL8 1AW. (£17.50)	01752 872372	555 487	58
*	*	*	Mrs Johnson, Crown Yealm, NEWTON FERRERS, Devon. (£17.00)	01752 872365		58
*	*	*	River Yealm Hotel, Yealm Road, NEWTON FERRERS, Devon, PL8 1BL. (£35.00)	01752 872419		58
*	*	*	Mrs L A Brunning, Netton Farm House, NOSS MAYO, Devon, PL8 1HA (will pick up). (£17.50)	01752 873080	537 471	58
*	*	*	Mr F A Gregory, Little Lawford Cottage, Bridgend, NOSS MAYO, Devon, PL8 1DX. (£12.50)	01752 872521	554 478	58
*	*	*	Mrs A Hill, Rowden House, Stoke Road, NOSS MAYO, Devon, PL8 1JG. (£15.00)	01752 872153	555 471	58
*	*	*	Mr Steer, Rookery Nook, Hannaford, NOSS MAYO, Plymouth, Devon. (£15.00)	01752 872296		58
*	*	*	Mrs E Wallis, Windlestraw, Penquit, ERMINGTON, Devon, PL21 0LU. (Erme, Avon and Yealm estuaries – will pick up and return). (£15.00)	01752 896237	646 544	57/58
*	*	*	Mr N Kies, Torr House, KINGSTON, Kingsbridge, Devon, TQ7 4PT. (£15.00)	01548 810723	640 480	58
*	*	*	D R Kinder, Trebles Cottage Hotel, KINGSTON, Devon TQ7 4PT. (£22.50)	01548 810268	640 480	58
*	*	*	Mrs P Brunskill, Cliff Path, RINGMORE, Kingsbridge, Devon, TQ7 4HR. (£13.00)	01548 810654	651 456	58
*	*	*	Mrs I Dodds, Ayrmer House, RINGMORE, Near Kingsbridge, Devon. (£17.00)	01548 810391		58
	*		Mrs B Evans, Merrylees, Ringmore Drive, BIGBURY ON SEA, Devon, TQ7 4AU. (£16.00)	01548 810247		58

P	O	D	Name and Address	Telephone No.	Map Ref.	Section
*	*	*	Mr & Mrs G Fortune, The Kashhu, Cleveland Drive, BIGBURY, Devon, TQ7 4AX. (£12.50)	01548 810584		58
*	*	*	Mrs B Lee, Rosebank, Folly Hill, BIGBURY ON SEA, Devon, TQ7 4AR. (£16.00)	01548 810724	653 444	58
*	*	*	Mr M Scarterfield, Henley Hotel, Folly Hill, BIGBURY ON SEA, Devon, TQ7 4AR. (£25.00)	01548 810240	657 444	58
*	*	*	Mr P J Sanders, Heron House Hotel, THURLESTONE SANDS, Devon. (£20.00)	01548 561308	676 412	59
*		*	Mr & Mrs N Upsdale, La Mer Hotel, THURLESTONE SANDS, Devon, TQ7 3JY. (on the path). (£15.00)	01548 561207	675 412	59
	*	*	Mr & Mrs W Hewitt, Rockcliffe, HOPE COVE, Devon. TQ7 3HG. (£16.50)	01548 560061		59
			Mrs G Idris, May Villa, Inner Hope Cove, HOPE COVE, Near Kingsbridge, Devon.TQ7 3HP. (£14.00)	01548 561887		59
*	*	*	Mr & Mrs R Petty-Brown, Rocarno, Grenville Road, SALCOMBE, Devon, TQ8 8BJ. (£13.00)	01548 842732	735 389	60
*	*	*	Mr & Mrs Axtell, Amalfi, Grenville Road, SALCOMBE, Devon. (£15.00)	01548 842155	735 389	60
*	*	*	Mrs C Jeyes, Beadon Farmhouse, Beadon Road, SALCOMBE, Devon, TQ8 8LX. (£16.00)	01548 843020	731 389	60
*		*	Lyndhurst Hotel, Bonaventure Road, SALCOMBE, Devon, TQ8 8BG. (£20.00)	01548 842481		60
*		*	Terrapins Hotel, Buckley, SALCOMBE, Devon. TQ8 8DD. (£25.00)	01548 842861		60
*		*	Torre View Hotel, Devon Road, SALCOMBE, Devon, TQ8 8HJ. (£22.50)	01548 842633	735 385	60
*		*	Trennels Hotel, Herbert Road, SALCOMBE, Devon, TQ8 8HR. (£19.00)	01548 842500		60
			Tourist Information Centre, Council Hall, Market Street, SALCOMBE, Devon, TQ8 8QL.	01548 842736		60
*	*	*	Mr & Mrs D Griffiths, Meadow Barn, High House, EAST PORTLEMOUTH, Nr. Salcombe, Devon, TQ8 8PN. (£16.00)	01548 843085	759 376	61
*	*	*	A & M Catt, Migrants Rest, EAST PRAWLE, Nr. Kingsbridge, Devon, TQ7 2DB. (£13.00)	01548 511443	779 366	61
*		*	M & L Davies, Maelcombe House, EAST PRAWLE, Devon, TQ7 2DE. (£15.50)	01548 511300	791 364	61
*	*	*	Hallsand Hotel, Hallsands, TORCROSS, Devon, TQ7 2EY. (£18.00)	01548 51264	818 388	61

P	O	D	Name and Address	Telephone No.	Map Ref.	Section
*	*	*	Mrs V J Mercer, Old Walls, Slapton, TORCROSS, Devon, TQ7 2QN. (£13.50)	01548 580516	822 449	61
*	*	*	Mr K Small, The Cove Guest House, TORCROSS, Kingsbridge, Devon, TQ7 2TH. (£18.00)	01548 580448	823 419	61
*	*	*	L Nixon, Southfield House, STOKE FLEMING, Devon, TQ6 0NR. (£18.00)	01803 770359	864 483	61
*	*	*	Mr B Dash, Britannia, 19 Clarence Street, DARTMOUTH, Devon, TQ6 9NW. (£14.00)	01803 833069		62
			Tourist Information Centre, Newcomen Engine House, Mayors Avenue, DARTMOUTH, Devon, TQ6 9YY.	01803 834224		62
	*	*	Mr I Hayhurst, Richmond House, Higher Manor Road, BRIXHAM, Devon, TQ5 8HA. (£15.00)	01803 882391	921 561	63
	*		Sampford House, 57/59 King Street, BRIXHAM, Devon, TQ5 9TH. (£15.00)	01803 857761		63
			Tourist Information Centre, The Quay, BRIXHAM, Devon, TQ5 8TB.	01803 852861		63
*		*	Mrs P Kingdom, Bruce Lodge Guest House, 2 Elmsleigh Road, PAIGNTON, Devon, TQ4 5AU. (£12.00)	01803 550972		64
*	*	*	Mrs M McHolm, 5a Fortescue Road, PAIGNTON, Devon, TQ3 3BZ. (£10.00)	01803 550667	894 616	64
*	*	*	Mrs P Whitlam, Cheltor Hotel, 20 St Andrews Road, PAIGNTON, Devon, TQ4 6HA. (£12.00)	01803 551507	891 602	64
			Tourist Information Centre, Festival Hall, Esplanade Road, PAIGNTON, Devon.	01803 558383		64
*	*	*	Mr D Day, Sunray Hotel, Aveland Road, Babbacombe, TORQUAY, Devon, TQ1 3PT. (£15.00)	01803 328285		64
*	*	*	Mr & Mrs J Rothwell, Suite Dreams, Steep Hill, Maidencombe, TORQUAY, Devon, TQ1 4TS. (£17.50)	01803 313900	927 685	64
	*	*	Mrs Sibthorp, The Beehive, Steep Hill, Maidencombe, TORQUAY, Devon, TQ1 4TS. (£15.00)	01803 314647		64
			Tourist Information Centre, Vaughan Parade, TORQUAY, Devon.	01803 297428		64
*	*	*	Glenside Hotel, Ringmore Road, SHALDON, Devon, TQ14 0EP. (£18.00)	01626 872448		65
*	*	*	London Hotel, Bank Street, TEIGNMOUTH, Devon, TQ14 8AW.	01626 776336	954 748	66
			Tourist Information Centre, The Den, TEIGNMOUTH, Devon, TQ14 8BE.	01626 779769		66
*	*	*	Mr & Mrs D Badcock, West Hatch Hotel, 34 West Cliff, DAWLISH, Devon, EX7 9DN (on Teignmouth Rd.). (£18.00)	01626 864211		66

P	O	D	Name and Address	Telephone No.	Map Ref.	Section
*	*	*	Mrs M Crouch, Glendora, Hall Lane, Holcombe, DAWLISH, Devon, EX7 0JP. (£15.00)	01626 864119	954 748	66
			Tourist Information Centre, The Lawn, DAWLISH, Devon, EX7 9AP.	01626 863589		66
	*	*	Mrs M Hayes, The Old Vicarage, STARCROSS, Nr. Exeter, Devon, EX6 8PX. (£14.50)	01626 890206		66
*	*	*	Barn Hotel, Foxholes Hill, EXMOUTH, Devon, EX8 2DF. (£32.00)	01395 224411		66
		*	Mrs Shobrook, 30 Withycombe Road, EXMOUTH, Devon, EX8 1TG. (£14.00)	01395 277025		66
			Tourist Information Centre, Alexandra Terrace, EXMOUTH, Devon, EX8 1NZ.	01395 263744		66
	*	*	Mrs Fletcher, The White Cottage, 25 East Budleigh Road, BUDLEIGH SALTERTON, Devon, EX9 6EJ. (£15.00)	01395 443574		67
*	*	*	Mrs S Freeman, 10 Knowle Village, BUDLEIGH SALTERTON, Devon. (£14.50)	01395 445807	050 825	67
			Tourist Information Centre, Fore Street, BUDLEIGH SALTERTON, Devon, EX9 6NG.	01395 445275		67
*	*	*	J Lee, Chapter House, 6 Westbourne Terrace, BUDLEIGH SALTERTON, Devon, EX9 6BR. (£15.00)	01395 444100		67
*	*	*	Diana Lee, Cheriton Guest House, 1 Elysian Villas, Vicarage Road, SIDMOUTH, Devon. (£14.00)	01395 513810		68
		*	Mrs L Lever, Canterbury House, Salcombe Road, SIDMOUTH, Devon, EX10 8PR. (£16.00)	01395 513373		68
			Tourist Information Centre, Ham Lane, SIDMOUTH, Devon, EX10 8XR.	01395 516441		68
*	*	*	Mr & Mrs R Hart, Hole Mill, BRANSCOMBE, Nr. Seaton, Devon, EX12 3BX.	01297 680314	193 895	69
*	*	*	The Dolphin Hotel, Fore Street, BEER, Devon, EX12 3EQ. (£15.00)	01297 20068		69
*	*	*	Mr M Christopher, Mariners Hotel, The Esplanade, SEATON, Devon, EX12 2NP. (£23.00)	01297 20560		69
*	*	*	Tors Guest House, 55 Harbour Road, SEATON, Devon, EX12 2LX. (£17.00)	01297 20531		69
			Tourist Information Centre (Seasonal), The Esplanade, SEATON, Devon.	01297 21689/21660		69

DORSET

P	O	D	Name and Address	Telephone No.	Map Ref.	Section
*		*	Ms M Bolton, Cliff Cottage Tea Garden, Cobb Road, LYME REGIS, Dorset, DT7 3JP. (£14.50)	01297 443334		70
*	*	*	Mr & Mrs D Brown, Old Monmouth Hotel, 12 Church Street, LYME REGIS, Dorset, DT7 3BS. (£15.00)	01297 442456	344 923	70

100

P	O	D	Name and Address	Telephone No.	Map Ref.	Section
*		*	Mrs J Harding, Coverdale Guest House, Woodmead Road, LYME REGIS, Dorset. (£12.00)	01297 442882	338 925	70
			Tourist Information Centre, Guildhall Cottage, Church Street, LYME REGIS, Dorset, DT7 3QA.	01297 442138		70
*	*	*	Mrs M Ward, Springfield House, Axminster Road, CHARMOUTH, Dorset, DT6 6PB. (£15.50)	01297 60509	361 937	71
*	*	*	Mr K A Baylis, Seatown Cottage, SEATOWN, Nr. Bridport, Dorset, DT6 6JT. (£14.00)	01297 89027	420 919	72
*	*	*	Mrs V Vallard, Egdon, Third Cliff Walk, WEST BAY, Dorset, DT6 4HX. (£12.50)	01308 422542	456 907	72
*	*	*	Mr & Mrs G Barnes, Broadstone Barn, Walditch, BRIDPORT, Dorset, DT6 4LA. (free pick-up). (£17.50)	01308 427430	484 927	72
	*	*	Mrs D Loving, 144 West Bay Road, BRIDPORT, Dorset, DT6 4AZ. (£15.00)	01308 422577	465 921	72
			Tourist Information Centre, 32 South Street, BRIDPORT, Dorset, DT6 3NO.	01309 24901		72
*	*	*	Mrs M Harman, Linton Cottage, ABBOTSBURY, Dorset, DT3 4JL. (£17.50)	01305 871339		73
*	*	*	Mrs W M Wood, East Farm, ABBOTSBURY, Dorset, DT3 4JN. (£15.00)	01305 871363		73
*	*	*	Mrs J Baker, Aveswood, 5 Bramdon Lane, PORTESHAM, Nr. Weymouth, Dorset DT3 4HG. (£16.00)	01305 871413	603 856	74
*	*	*	Mrs S A Andrews, Foxbarrow House, LANGTON HERRING, Nr. Weymouth, Dorset, DT3 4HT. (£15.00)	01305 871463	614 825	74
	*		Mrs P Westcott, Stonebank, 14 West Street, CHICKERELL, Nr. Weymouth, Dorset, DT3 4DY. (£17.50)	01305 760120	807 643	74
*	*	*	Mr & Mrs D J Boucher, Southbrook, Preston Road, Overcombe, WEYMOUTH, Dorset, DT3 6PU. (£17.50)	01305 832208	697 821	74
	*	*	Mrs M Wakefield, Anchorage, 23 Stavordale Road, WEYMOUTH, Dorset, DT4 0AB. (£15.00)	01305 785719	675 792	74
*	*	*	Westwey Hotel, 62 Abbotsbury Road, WEYMOUTH, Dorset. (£15.50)	01305 784564		74
*	*	*	Mr & Mrs G Wincott, Florian, 59 Abbotsbury Road, Westham, WEYMOUTH, Dorset, DT4 0AQ. (£13.00)	01305 773836	667 792	74
			Tourist Information Centre, The Esplanade, WEYMOUTH Dorset, DT4 8ED.	01305 765221/765223		74
	*		Mrs K Legg, Rosedale, Church Lane, OSMINGTON, Near Weymouth, Dorset, DT3 6EW. (£12.00)	01305 832056	725 830	75
*	*	*	Ms B Leigh, Rosthwaite, Church Lane, OSMINGTON, Dorset, DT3 6EW. (£14.00)	01305 833621	725 830	75

P	O	D	Name and Address	Telephone No.	Map Ref.	Section
*	*	*	R & D Foote, Lulworth Cove Hotel, WEST LULWORTH, Wareham, Dorset, BH20 5RQ. (on the path). (£16.00)	01929 400333		75
*	*	*	Mrs C Miller, Cromwell House Hotel, WEST LULWORTH, Wareham, Dorset, BH20 5RJ. (£24.50)	01929 400253	823 801	75
*		*	Shirley Hotel, WEST LULWORTH, Wareham, Dorset, BH20 5RL. (£25.00)	01929 400358	824 806	75
*	*	*	P & L Simpson, Newland Farm, WEST LULWORTH, Wareham, Dorset, BH20 5PU. (£18.00)	01929 400376	810 810	75
*	*	*	Mrs G Hole, Bradle Farm, Church Knowle, KIMMERIDGE, Dorset, BH20 5NU. (£16.00)	01929 480712	930 805	76
*	*	*	Mrs A Hole, Kimmeridge Farm House, KIMMERIDGE, Dorset, BH20 5PE. (£16.00)	01929 480990	916 799	76
*	*	*	Ms C Cruse, Kingsley Hall Hotel, 8 Ulwell Road, SWANAGE, Dorset, BH19 1LH. (in town). (£25.00)	01929 422872		77
*	*	*	C & J Davison, Penny Farthings, 124 Kings Road West, SWANAGE, Dorset, BH19 1HS. (£14.00)	01929 422256	023 789	77
	*		Mr & Mrs A Preston, The Corner House, 4 Manor Road, SWANAGE, Dorset, BH19 2BJ. (£13.00)	01929 424410	031 785	77
	*	*	Esme Prior, Belros, WORTH MATRAVERS, Swanage, Dorset. (£18.00)	01929 439259	973 773	77
*		*	Skelmorlie House, 50 Queens Road, SWANAGE, Dorset, BH19 2EU. (£15.00)	01929 423643	031 784	77
	*		West Country Hotel, 12 Rempstone Road, SWANAGE, Dorset, BH19 1DW. (£19.50)	01929 423271	030 790	77
	*		Mrs B Willey, Verulam Lodge, 26 Cluny Crescent, SWANAGE, Dorset, BH19 2BT. (£14.50)	01929 422079	032 784	77
			Tourist Information Centre, The White House, Shore Road, SWANAGE, Dorset, BH19 1LB.	01929 422885		77
*	*		Mrs North, The Laurels, 60 Britannia Road, POOLE, Dorset, BH14 8BB. (£16.00)	01202 723369	033 913	78
			Tourist Information Centre, The Quay, POOLE, Dorset, BH15 1HE.	01202 673322		78

YOUTH HOSTEL ASSOCIATION – ACCOMMODATION ADDRESSES

There is an amazing variety of Youth Hostels along the South West Way, 24 in total and all offering comfortable, friendly accommodation. Prices start from £3.60 per night including bed linen, the use of self-catering kitchens, drying rooms and cycle sheds. The YHA is a membership organisation, non members are welcome to join on arrival at the Youth Hostel. Membership (annual £3 Under 18 – £9 Adults) enables you to take advantage of the 5000 Youth Hostels world wide, regular member's magazine 'Triangle', annual YHA Accommodation Guides and discounts at YHA Adventure Shops and local tourist attractions. The meals are excellent value, Breakfast £2.70, Packed Lunch £2.20–3.00, Evening Meal £4.00.

Book directly with the Youth Hostel of your choice or for further assistance please contact South England Regional Office, 11b York Road, Salisbury, Wiltshire, SP2 7AP. Tel: 01722 337494.

Prices range from £3.60 to £8.80 and are for bed and bed linen, available on application to each Hostel.

P	O	D	Name and Address	Telephone No.	Map Ref.	Section
			SOMERSET			
*		*	Minehead Youth Hostel, Alcombe Combe, Minehead, TA24 6EW	Minehead (01643) 702595	973 442	1
			NORTH DEVON			
*		*	Lynton Youth Hostel, Lynbridge, Lynton, EX35 6AZ.	Lynton (01598) 53237	720 487	2
*		*	Ilfracombe Youth Hostel, Ashmour House, 1 Hillsborough Tce., Ilfracombe, EX34 9NR.	Ilfracombe (01271) 865337	524 476	4
*		*	Instow Youth Hostel, Worlington House, New Road,Instow, Bideford, EX39 4LW.	Instow (01271) 860394	482 303	9
		*	Elmscott Youth Hostel, Hartland, Bideford, EX39 6ES. (Self catering only)	Hartland (01237) 441367	231 217	11
			CORNWALL			
*		*	Boscastle Youth Hostel, Palace Stables, Boscastle, PL35 0HD.	Boscastle (01840) 250287	096 915	14
		*	Tintagel Youth Hostel, Dunderhole Point, Tintagel, PL34 0DW. (Self catering only)	Tintagel (01840) 770334	047 881	15
*		*	Treyarnon Youth Hostel, Tregonnan, Treyarnon, Padstow PL28 8JR.	Padstow (01841) 520322	859 741	19
*		*	Perranporth Youth Hostel, Droskyn Point, Perranporth, TR6 0DS. (Self catering only)	Truro (01872) 573812	752 544	23
*		*	Land's End Youth Hostel, Letcha Vean, St Just-in-Penwith, Penzance, TR19 7NT.	Penzance (01736) 788437	364 305	30
*	*	*	Penzance Youth Hostel, Castle Horneck, Alverton, Penzance, TR20 8TF.	Penzance (01736) 62666	457 302	34
*		*	Coverack Youth Hostel, Park Behan, School Hill, Coverack, Helston, TR12 6SA.	St Keverne (01326) 280687	782 181	40
*		*	Pendennis Castle Youth Hostel, Pendennis Castle, Falmouth, TR11 4LP.	Falmouth (01326) 311435	823 319	42
*		*	Boswinger Youth Hostel, Boswinger, Gorran, St Austell, PL26 6LL.	Mevagissey (01726) 843234	991 411	49
*		*	Golant Youth Hostel, Penquite House, Golant, Fowey, PL23 1LA	Fowey (01726) 833507	118 557	51

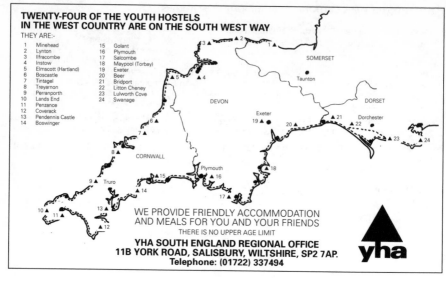

TWENTY-FOUR OF THE YOUTH HOSTELS IN THE WEST COUNTRY ARE ON THE SOUTH WEST WAY

THEY ARE:-

1	Minehead	15	Golant
2	Lynton	16	Plymouth
3	Ilfracombe	17	Salcombe
4	Instow	18	Maypool (Torbay)
5	Elmscott (Hartland)	19	Exeter
6	Boscastle	20	Beer
7	Tintagel	21	Bridport
8	Treyarnon	22	Litton Cheney
9	Perranporth	23	Lulworth Cove
10	Lands End	24	Swanage
11	Penzance		
12	Coverack		
13	Pendennis Castle		
14	Boswinger		

WE PROVIDE FRIENDLY ACCOMMODATION
AND MEALS FOR YOU AND YOUR FRIENDS
THERE IS NO UPPER AGE LIMIT
**YHA SOUTH ENGLAND REGIONAL OFFICE
11B YORK ROAD, SALISBURY, WILTSHIRE, SP2 7AP.
Telephone: (01722) 337494**

P	O	D	Name and Address	Telephone No.	Map Ref.	Section
			SOUTH DEVON			
*		*	Plymouth Youth Hostel, Belmont House, Belmont Place, Stoke, Plymouth, PL3 4DW.	Plymouth (01752) 562189	461 555	55
*		*	Salcombe Youth Hostel, 'Overbecks', Sharpitor, Salcombe, TQ8 8LW.	Salcombe (0154884) 2856	728 374	60
*		*	Maypool Youth Hostel, Maypool House, Galmpton, Brixham, TQ5 0ET.	Churston (01803) 842444	877 546	64
*		*	Exeter Youth Hostel 47–49 Countess Wear Road, Exeter, EX2 6LR	Exeter (01392) 873329	942 897	66/67
*		*	Beer Youth Hostel, Bovey Combe, Townsend, Beer, Seaton, EX12 3LL.	Seaton (01297) 20296	223 896	69
			DORSET			
*		*	BridportYouth Hostel, West Rivers House, West Allington, Bridport, DT6 5BW.	Bridport (01308) 422655	461 930	72
*		*	Litton CheneyYouth Hostel, Litton Cheney, Dorchester, DT2 9AT. (No smoking hostel.)	Long Bredy (01308) 482340	548 900	74
*		*	Lulworth Cove Youth Hostel, School Lane, West Lulworth, Wareham, BH20 5SA.	W. Lulworth (01929) 400564	832 806	75
*		*	Swanage Youth Hostel, Cluny, Cluny Cresc., Swanage, BH19 2BS.	Swanage (01929) 422113	030 785	77

CAMPING

A list of Camp Sites has been prepared in path order anti-clockwise. Useful information and free leaflets can also be obtained as follows:

The Exmoor Visitor 1995: A free comprehensive guide (including accommodation). Please apply to Department E.V., Exmoor National Park Authority, Exmoor House, Dulverton, Somerset TA22 9HL.

Tourist Officer, Cornwall County Council, County Hall, Truro.

Devon County Tourist Officer, County Hall, Topsham Road, Exeter.

County Public Relations & Information Officer, County Hall, Dorchester, Dorset DT1 1XJ.

Individuals – but we stress **not parties** – usually find no problem in obtaining leave to camp away from official camp sites if they request permission to do so. In fact, our correspondence has many examples of extra kindnesses extended by farmers and others to campers. We would, however, very much emphasize the requesting of permission first. It would be so easy for the thoughtless-ness of a few to undo the good relationships of many others built up over some years.

This list is thin in many areas. Suggestions for inclusions in future lists will always be welcome. Information of any new sites should be addressed to the Membership Secretary.

Name and Address	Telephone No.	Map Ref.	Site Open (Dates inclusive)	Section
NORTH DEVON				
Newberry Campsite, Woodlands, COMBE MARTIN, Devon, EX34 0AT.	01271 882333/4	576 473	April – October	3
Hele Valley Holiday Park, Hele Bay, ILFRACOMBE, Devon, EX34 9RD.	01271 862460		April – October	4
Croyde Bay Holidays, Croyde Bay, Moore Lane, CROYDE Nr. Braunton Devon, EX33 1NZ.	01271 890351	437 395	Easter – October	7
Mr G J Reynolds, Pusehill Farm, WESTWARD HO Nr. Bideford, Devon, EX39 5AH.	01237 474295	427 283	Easter – September	9
Mrs J Johns, Dyke Green Farm Camping Site, HIGHER CLOVELLY, Nr. Bideford, Devon, EX39 5RU.	01237 431279	311 237	March – October	10
C J Davey, Stoke Barton Farm, HARTLAND, Near Bideford, Devon, EX39 6DU.	01237 441238	234 246	March – October	11
Mrs Cornish, Leddon Farm, Darracott, WELCOMBE, Bideford, Devon.	01288 331380	231 178	All year	12
NORTH CORNWALL				
Wooda Farm Caravan & Camping Park, Wooda Farm, POUGHILL, Bude, Cornwall, EX23 9HJ.	01288 352069	229 078	Easter – October	12

Name and Address	Telephone No.	Map Ref.	Site Open (Dates inclusive)	Section
Upper Lynstone Camping & Caravan Park, BUDE, Cornwall, EX23 0LP.	01288 352017	205 053	Easter – End September	12
Mrs S Weller, Hentervene C & C Park, CRACKINGTON HAVEN, Near Bude, Cornwall, EX23 0LF.	01840 230365	155 944	All year	13
Mr & Mrs M Francis, The Headland Caravan & Camping Park, Atlantic Road, TINTAGEL, Cornwall, PL34 0DE.	01840 770239		Easter – October 31	15
Little Bodieve Holiday Park, WADEBRIDGE, Cornwall, PL27 6EG	01208 812323		Mid March – October	17/18
Dennis Cove Campsite, Dennis Cove, PADSTOW, Cornwall, PL28 8DR.	01841 532349	920 745	Easter – 30 September	18
Carnevas Farm Holiday Park, PORTHCOTHAN BAY, Nr. St Merryn, Cornwall, PL28 8PN	01841 520230	863 725	April – End October	20
Trevornick Holiday Park, HOLYWELL BAY, Newquay, Cornwall.	01637 830531		1st May – 30th September	21
Trevella Caravan & Camping Park, CRANTOCK, Newquay, Cornwall, TR8 5EW.	01637 830308		Open all year	22
Beacon Cottage Farm Touring Park, Beacon Drive, ST AGNES, Cornwall, TR5 0NU.	01872 552347	705 505	May – October	24
H Williams, Manor Farm, Tehidy PORTREATH, Camborne, Cornwall.	01209 713367	632 427	March – October	26
Mr C White, St Ives Bay Holiday Park, 73 Loggans Road, HAYLE, Cornwall, TR27 5BH.	01736 752274		1 May – 30 September	27
Mr M Osborne, Trevalgan Family Camping Park, ST IVES, Cornwall, TR26 3BJ.	01736 796433	490 402	May – End September	28
Kelynack Caravan & Camping Park, Kelynack, ST JUST, Penzance. Cornwall	01736 787633	374 301	Bunkhouse now open Easter – End October	29

SOUTH CORNWALL

Name and Address	Telephone No.	Map Ref.	Site Open (Dates inclusive)	Section
Treen Campsite, Treen, ST LEVAN, Nr. Penzance. Cornwall.	01736 810526	392 228	April – End October	33
Bone Valley Caravan Park, Heamoor, PENZANCE, Cornwall, TR20 8UJ.	01736 60313	462 318	March – mid December	34

Name and Address	Telephone No.	Map Ref.	Site Open (Dates inclusive)	Section
Wheal Rodney, Gwallon, MARAZION, Cornwall TR17 0HL.	01736 710605		April – October	35
Tenerife Farm Caravan & Campsite, Attn. A.B. Thomas, Predannack, MULLION. Cornwall.	01326 240293	677 172	Easter – End October	38
Criggan Mill, MULLION COVE, Cornwall, TR12 7EU.	01326 240496	671 178	April – October	38
Silver Sands Holiday Park, Gwendreath, KENNACK SANDS, Helston, Cornwall, TR12 7LZ.	01326 290631	729 169	Early April – End September	40
Gwendreath Farm Caravan Park, KENNACK SANDS, Helston, Cornwall, TR12 7LZ.	01326 290666	729 167	Easter – October	40
Tremorvah Tent Park, Swanpool, FALMOUTH, Cornwall, TR11 5BE.	01326 312103	799 312	May – End September	42
J B Jewell, Pennance Mill Farm, Maenporth, FALMOUTH. Cornwall, TR11 5HJ.	01326 312616	791 307	Easter – End October	42
Trewince Manor, Trewince, PORTSCATHO, Truro, Cornwall, TR2 5ET.	01872 580289	868 338	Open all year	44
Trelispen Camping Park, GORRAN HAVEN, Cornwall.	01726 843501	005 421	Easter – End October	47
Sun Valley Holiday Park, Pentewan Road, ST AUSTELL, Cornwall, PL26 6DJ.	01726 843266		April – End October	50
Carlyon Bay Camping Park, Cypress Avenue, Carlyon Bay, CHARLESTOWN, Nr. St Austell, Cornwall, PL25 3RE.	01726 812735	053 525	Easter – September	50

SOUTH DEVON

Name and Address	Telephone No.	Map Ref.	Site Open (Dates inclusive)	Section
Higher Rew Farm Camping Park, MARLBOROUGH, Nr. Salcombe, Devon, TQ7 3DW.	01548 842681	714 383	Easter – October	60
Camping & Caravanning Club Site, Middle Grounds, Slapton, TORCROSS. Devon, TQ6 1QW.	01548 580538	825 450	Mid March – September	61/62

Name and Address	Telephone No.	Map Ref.	Site Open (Dates inclusive)	Section
Leonards Cove, Stoke Fleming, DARTMOUTH, Devon, TQ6 0NR.	01803 770206	864 483	March – October	62
W & J Hosking, Upton Manor Farm Camping, St Mary's Road, BRIXHAM, Devon, TQ5 9QH.	01803 882384	549 926 path 1/2 mile	May 25 – September 10th	63
Beverly Park Holiday Park, Goodrington Road, PAIGNTON. Devon, TQ4 7JE	01803 843887	886 582	1st April – 31st October	64
Marine Park Holiday Centre, Garage Road, PAIGNTON, Devon, TQ4 7JR	01803 843887	886 587	1 May – 30 September	64
Cofton Farm Caravan & Camping Park, Starcross, Nr. DAWLISH. Devon.	01626 890358		Easter – End October	66
Ladram Bay Caravan Site, LADRAM BAY, Nr. Budleigh Salterton, BUDLEIGH. Devon. EX9 7BX	01395 568395	096 845	April – End September	68
Oakdown Caravan Parks, Weston, SIDMOUTH, Devon, EX10 0PH.	01297 680387	167 902	April – October	68
Manor Farm Camping & Caravan Site, Seaton Down Hill, SEATON, Devon, EX12 2JA.	01297 21524		March 1st – November 1st	69

DORSET

Name and Address	Telephone No.	Map Ref.	Site Open (Dates inclusive)	Section
Newlands Camping Park, CHARMOUTH, Dorset, DT6 6RB	01297 560259	373 935	16 March – 31 October	71
Manor Farm Holiday Centre, CHARMOUTH, Dorset, DT6 6QL.	01297 560226		All year	71
Wood Farm Caravan & Camping Park, Axminster Road, CHARMOUTH, Dorset, DT6 6BT.	01297 560697	355 940	April – October	71
Golden Cap Holiday Park, Seatown, CHIDEOCK, Bridport, Dorset, DT6 6AR.	01308 422139	422 919	March – October	72
Mr K G Mundy, Eype House Caravan & Camping Park, EYPE, Nr. Bridport,Dorset, DT6 6AL.	01308 424903	446 912	Easter Mid October	72
Freshwater Holiday Park, BURTON BRADSTOCK, Nr. Bridport. Dorset, DTS 4PT	01308 897317	898 479	13 March – 1 November	73
Sea Barn Farm Camping, Fleet, WEYMOUTH, Dorset, DT3 4ED.	01305 782218		Easter – October	74

Name and Address	Telephone No.	Map Ref.	Site Open (Dates inclusive)	Section
Pebble Bank Caravan Park, 90 Camp Road, Wyke Regis, WEYMOUTH, Dorset, DT4 9HF.	01305 774844	657 775	April – October	74
Osmington Mills Holidays Ltd. The Ranch House, OSMINGTON MILLS, Dorset, DT3 6HB.	01305 832311	733 822	Easter – End of September	75
Osmington Mills Holidays, East Farm Dairy Camping Park, The Ranch House, OSMINGTON MILLS, Dorset, DT3 6HB.	01305 83231	735 823	Easter – October	75
Durdle Door Caravan Park, Lulworth Cove, WEST LULWORTH, Dorset, BH20 5PU	01929 400 200	811 808	March – End October	75

SOUTH WEST WAY ASSOCIATION – HISTORY

We are sometimes asked what we have done and we set out below some of the things in which we have been involved in one way or another. We do as well send a steady flow of reports on path deficiencies, both as regards maintenance and the route of the path to the local authorities and the Countryside Commission.

1973   Official Formation in May.
Attendance Cornish Opening at Newquay.
Comments to Sports Council on proposed Countryside Park at Northam Burrows.
First Information Sheets produced.

1974   Evidence submitted to Mr Yapp for his report to the Countryside Commission on Long Distance Footpaths.
We welcomed Devon N.F.U. representation on our Committee.
Attendance at South Devon and Dorset Opening in September at Beer.
Registration as a Charity.
First Description issued.

1975   Mark Richard's book "Walking the North Cornwall Coastal Path" published – a work in which we may fairly say we played a part.
Small new section of Coast Path agreed at Clematon Hill, Bigbury at S.W.W.A.'s instigation.
Article on S.W.W. in Rucksack.
Attendance at Opening of so-called Exmoor Coastal Path.
Bideford Public Enquiry – successful opposition to Golf Course on the Coastal Path at Abbotsham.
Success at last in getting path south from Hartland Point over Blagdon and Upright Cliffs.
Walk over new Lulworth Range Walk.

1976   First Footpath Guide issued.
Diversion at Thurlestone opposed.
Evidence submitted to House of Commons Expenditure Committee Environment sub-committee.
Improvements at North Cliffs between Portreath and Hayle secured, thanks to National Trust.
Public Enquiry with R.A. at Kingswear on the section Kellys Cove to Mann Sands.
Consulted by Devon County Council on path at Watermouth and Dorset County Council about Abbotsbury.
Goodbye to our first Chairman, Mr Walter – we lose a tower of strength.

1977   S.W.W.A. mentioned in the Y.H. Handbook.
Publications of Letts Guides in three volumes. The first satisfactory books to whole path in which we can say our information helped a little.
Attendance at Coverack Youth Hostel official opening.
Evidence presented to Lord Porchester's Exmoor Study.
Badges produced.
Evidence given to Devon County Council for Taw/Torridge Estuary Survey.

1978   First Printed Footpath guide.
Attendance at Westward Ho! Somerset/North Devon Opening.
Opposition to diversion at Dean Quarry, St Keverne, Cornwall.
Lack of Path at Pentewan submitted to Local Ombudsman.
New path seaward of Radar Station at Hartland obtained, thanks to South West Way Association.

1979   Evidence given at Public Enquiries at Abbotsbury and Lulworth Cove.
Submission to Mr Himsworth for his report on Areas of Outstanding Natural Beauty.
First printed News Letters and Descriptions, and the first illustrated description.
Pine Haven to Port Quin gap submitted to Local Ombudsman.
Assistance to Letts for their Guide reprint.

1980   Result of 1976 Public Enquiry at Kingswear published.
Discussion Dean Quarry, St Keverne, Cornwall.
Dialogues with Countryside Commission about path deficiencies.
Alternative coastal path open Glenthorne Estate, Somerset and we submit proposals for rerouting in Exmoor National Park.
Special report submitted on St Loy, Cornwall.
Attendance at Widmouth Head, North Devon, Public Enquiry.
Opinions expressed to Department of Environment on draft "Wildlife and Countryside Bill".

1981   Annual Guide "State of the Path" section improved.
Attendance at second Kingswear Public Enquiry.
Countryside Commission decide that path wardenship will be greatly extended.
Bridge provided at Duckpool, North Cornwall.
Path improvements at Watermouth; Braunton to Barnstaple; Dean Quarry; Clematon Hill; Bigbury; Mothecombe and Maidencombe.

1982   Wardenship of coastal path in Cornwall completed.
Further openings at: Cleave Farm in North Cornwall, Pentewan with its unfortunate execution and Mount Edgecombe in South Cornwall, Higher Brownstone Farm, Kingswear and a short section west of Berry Head in South Devon.
Agreement was also reached for a high tide route at Mothecombe in South Devon.
The 1982 Guide incorporates a new 'Itinerary Suggested' section.

1983   Opening of the Widmouth Head section in North Devon and a second long section in South Devon between Kingswear and Mann Sands.
Major improvements to the Path on the western side of Crackington Haven, North Cornwall.
Cornwall's 10th Anniversary Walk.

1984   **New Section**
A new section of the Path opened on the east bank of the mouth of the River Dart close to Kingswear and giving access to Mill Bay Cove and a splendid stretch of coastal walking.

Improvement
A coastal route was opened westwards from Trebarwith Strand to Backways Cove in North Cornwall.

1985   **Improvement**
There was an improvement to the Dawlish/Teignmouth section of the path between Smugglers Lane and Windward Lane where the path has been removed from the main road.

Culbone – Foreland Point
The alternative coastal path at the Glenthorne Estate was waymarked as the official route, which is a great improvement.

Pinehaven – Port Quin (North Cornwall)
The new path was opened and is a vast improvement, although the substantial fence and barbed wire detracts from the scene.

1986   **Minehead to Porlock Weir** New alternative path between North Hill and Hurlstone Point signposted and waymarked.

Black Head, Cornwall Now purchased by the National Trust.

1987   **Barnstaple/Bideford/Northam** The new route completed along the railway lines and open.

Bude Attendance at Public Enquiry to prevent development adjacent to footpath.

Chynhalls Point Coast path moved to seaward of hotel.

Branscombe Attendance at Public Enquiry to urge true coast path instead of inland route. Preferred route adopted.

Bidna/Northam Owing to breach in sea wall an acceptable diversion negotiated.

1988   **Woody Bay to Trentishoe** Devon County Council adopts our recommended, nearer the coast route as the official coast path.

1989   **Culbone** On site exploration with Countryside Commission and Exmoor National Park Authority to discover an acceptable alternative to the long unnecessary Culbone diversion.

Chynhalls Cliff On site exploration for a more coastal trail.

Fire Beacon Point/Pentargon Cornwall County Council install grand new path.

Wembury Attend public meeting at Down Thomas to successfully oppose erection of locked gates across Coast Path by Royal Navy.

Strete Gate/Warren Cove Attend public meeting and give evidence to support proposals by Countryside Commission and Devon County Council for an improved and more true coast path.

1990   **Membership** Now over 1000.

1991   **Buckator** At our request Cornwall County Council re-route offical path around the headland.

Worthy/Culbone On site explorations for a preferable diversion to that proposed by Exmoor National Park Authority.

Strete Gate/Warren Cove Continuing our strong argument with Devon County Council for a coast path.

Lyme Regis Continued pleas to Dorset County Council to reinstate the coast path along the golf course.

Total length we estimate the Coast Path to be about 613 miles long.

1992   Our recommended route between Watcombe and Maidencombe put in by Devon County Council.

Our suggested path at Worthygate Wood installed by National Trust.

Commenced discussions with Countryside Commission to examine sections of coast suitable for 'Set Aside'.

1993   Successful opposition to an application to close path on west side of Foreland Point.

Success with our request for a coast path avoiding the holiday complex at Buck's Mills.

Our suggested path installed by National Trust at Port Quin.

Write and produce the 'trail description' in this book the 'Other Way Round'.

1994   Invited by the Countryside Commission to become a member of the South West Coast Path Steering Group to review the management of our Coast Path.

INVITATION TO MEMBERSHIP

The South West Way is interesting in that it is not a modern idea like the Pennine Way; until 1913, it was an established working path patrolled on foot daily. The rows of coastguard cottages and old stone stiles remaining in many places are evidence of this usage. The Path when finished will run from Minehead in Somerset right round the South West Peninsula as far as Poole Harbour in Dorset. It will be the longest of the Long Distance Paths and more than twice the length of the Pennine Way – over 600 miles in fact.

The splendid idea of making this old path around the South West Peninsula one of the first of a series of Long Distance Paths came from a war-time committee of the Ramblers Association. The idea was put into effect by being included in the National Park and Access to the Countryside Act of 1949. In other words, Long Distance Footpaths have an equal basis in law with the much better known National Parks. Unfortunately, for the Long Distance Footpaths, they have largely been treated as poor relations ever since. The proof of this is, despite being authorised by Act of Parliament so long ago and despite several Opening Ceremonies, the South West Way is still unfinished.

The South West Way Association was formed after some months' preliminary work in May 1973. It is an independent body but works in co-operation with the Ramblers Association. The South West Way Association's first aim is to secure completion of the path, and we do believe we have been responsible for many path alignment improvements and better maintenance and waymarking during our 22 year existence.

Furthermore, the South West Way Association believe the Countryside Commission have been in error in two respects. Firstly, they have not made it a continuous path despite their own words: "There should be a continuous right of way along the entire length of the path." (Countryside Commission's National Long Distance Path – Some Questions Answered.)

Secondly, in several places, the Path has been diverted from the coast for no apparent good reason, even on occasions, on to main roads with no pavement. The South West Way Association believe it would be scenically more beautiful, less hindrance to agriculture and physically safer if kept on the coast. Experience has shown that diversions away from it are on the whole not satisfactory.

It seems that no local walking organizations were ever consulted about the path until South West Way Association came into being. Being reasonable people we cannot expect to have everything our own way – in fact there are many legitimate interests to consider. However, to establish a path without discussing it with the people who know it best, which is exactly what the Countryside Commission were apparently trying to do, seems altogether wrong.

The South West Way Association believe that, in a tourist-orientated area such as the South West, a continuous coastal path will be a major asset. It hopes the Path will bring more business to less frequented places and relieve some of the pressure on the South West National Parks. There are a great number of bodies interested in various parts of the Path. The South West Way Association believes it is important that it should represent all sections, and view the Path as a whole.

Members receive a free Annual Guide, two Newsletters a year with up-to-date information and a free copy of each new footpath description as it is issued.

Enquiries to: Mrs M. Macleod, Membership Secretary,

South West Way Association,

1 Orchard Drive, Kingskerswell, Newton Abbot,

Devon TQ12 5DG. Telephone: (01803) 873061

Subscriptions: £7.00; Joint £8.00

Associations, Local Authorities £12.00; Life Subscription £120.00;

Joint £140.00. Non-UK membership £10.00.